Circle of Life

Adrian Webster

EXCERPT FROM CIRCLE OF LIFE

I stood in the tunnel with my heart pounding and my stomach tied in knots. The chanting of the fans could be heard rocking the seats around us. All the other familiar sights and sounds faded. I was game ready. Focused. I had to be. My career was summed up in this moment. This was the Championship playoff game and I would come up against three World Cup Winners, Pele, Carlos Alberto and Franz Beckenbauer. Pele! The soccer player that still to this day is said to possibly be the greatest player of all time. Yes me, the boy from little old Colchester.

The cheers rose to a roar and flags waved in the stands. Since the game was only a couple of hours drive for our supporters, there seemed to be more local fans than for New York. As I and the lads strode out onto the pitch, I remember thinking this is for you, our fans, who started on the journey in 1974.

Copyright

Circle of Life
Books to Go Now Publication

FOREWORD

By David Falk of goalWA.net

Adrian Webster brought a great work ethic and passionate play to the NASL Sounders. Those were the days of playing at Memorial Stadium before sell-out crowds of 17,000 who literally hung over the field on those steeply-graded stands while hanging on every kick from the home side. It seems like a lifetime away, yet the memories are still fresh. Webster and his mates doing the impossible in 1977, a season that seemed to flat line but then turned into the Sounders first deep playoff run. 58,000 fans cheering as Jocky Scott headed home the winner and Adrian's club defeated the LA Aztecs and George Best. Then came the big day, an event which all true Sounders fans set their spiritual clocks by. Soccer Bowl 77 and Pele's last match, the league final against Webster's Sounders.

True to his role as captain Webster was a leader on the slick astroturf at bitter rival Portland's Civic Stadium. I wonder if he could have known that his tangles with Pele would be captured on film stock and preserved online for future generations. At the time it was all about stopping the World's greatest player and earning

Seattle a title. While Pele was held in check, the New York Cosmos managed a 2-1 win breaking the hearts of Adrian and his mates and thousands of traveling Seattle supporters. It mattered greatly at the time – it still does – and yet somehow over the years the bitterness of that loss has turned to a cherished snapshot of a lost time.

Maybe it is just like that with " first times. " It was Seattle's first league final. It was a first time to see Adrian Webster, Steve Buttle, Mike England the whole lot compete for a ring and a cup. They did not let Seattle down. It just wasn't meant to be. Seattle returned to the NASL Final in 1982 but it was already a different era. Webster was elsewhere but one thing remained the same. It was the Cosmos. It was another one goal loss.

Our brave Adrian, bearded and with the long hair so popular in the 1970's, was a player of control and physicality, of determination and desire. It was hard not to adopt these imported players when they so quickly earned and then kept our respect and loyalty. Off of the pitch they might have been on " holiday " in Seattle, cheerfully mingling with supporters at picnics and before and after matches...but on the field they were warriors, wearing our badge and fighting to make it there badge as well. So many, many memories and " victory laps " included Adrian and the fellows of his era. Most of them, like him, remember their days in Seattle with much fondness, as do many of us.

DEDICATION

Jenni and Bill Conner and the next generation Sounder fans,

their son Dalton and wife Amy.

I would like to dedicate this book to Jenni and Bill Conner. I first met Jenni during the 1976 season, our first season playing in the Kingdome. At the time Jenni was involved in her school photography program. In 1977 her dad drove her down to Portland for the Soccer Bowl Final and she was able to take some fantastic shots of that incredible game.

In 1979 while attending the Sounders game up in Vancouver she met Bill Conner and in May the following year they were married. Almost 38 years on they are still married and are still avid Sounders fans!

I met Bill in May 2017 when they visited England and my wife Jo and I were able to spend a lovely couple of days in London with them. During my recent visit to Seattle Jenni was very much involved in organizing the reunion with some of my former teammates for the 40th Anniversary of Soccer Bowl 77. During my visit I had a lovely lunch with Jenni, Bill, Dave and Linda Gillett and Dave Butler where Bill took us down memory lane with some of his old Sounders albums.

I would particularly like to thank Jenni for all the hard work and effort she has put into publishing my three books and for all the help, support and encouragement she has given me. Thanks Jenni for making it happen!

INTRODUCTION

By Adrian Webster

CIRCLE OF LIFE is a compilation of my two books Eternal Blue Forever Green and the 40th Anniversary Soccer Bowl 77 Seattle Sounders Vs New York Cosmos as well as all about my recent visit to Seattle where I received the Golden Scarf.

The purpose of my visit was to celebrate the 40th Anniversary of Soccer Bowl 77 Seattle Sounders Vs New York Cosmos, to promote my two books and to catch up with some old friends.

I was now visiting Seattle the home of the current MLS Champions, I had not been there in 26 years. The NASL had folded and the MLS did not exist. There had been a generation of young American soccer players who had missed the opportunity to play professional soccer and 40,000 plus fans who were waiting for a new pro team and to win a National Championship.

The current MLS Sounders started their 2016 season much like the 77 Sounders only this time they replaced their Head Coach Sigi Schmid with local boy Brian Schmetzer and as they say the rest is history as Brian went on to lead the team to a MLS Championship.

MY JOURNEY

My Soccer journey spans almost 50 years. A career that took me from my hometown Colchester to Vancouver Canada and then onto Seattle, Pittsburgh and Phoenix in the US and finally full circle back home to Colchester where I am now retired.

My first book Eternal Blue Forever Green came about after my former teammate and Sounders great Alan Hudson asked me to contribute a couple of pieces for a book he was writing. Doing it really got my juices flowing and I began tapping out more and more memories of my own six seasons playing for the Sounders (74-79). I had never really thought about writing my own book, although I had often thought how neat it would be to do something I could pass onto my grandchildren.

If someone had said to me when I left school aged 16 I would still be involved in football when I was 63 I would probably have fallen over laughing! When I started writing Eternal Blue Forever Green I was off work, the result of all those years of kicking a soccer ball and a few opponents. I had just had surgery on my other big toe which left me on crutches for six weeks and with plenty of time to take a trip down memory lane.

When I first got into professional football in the late 60's it was never about an ambition to make lots of money but more about a way to earn a living while doing something I loved to do. Subsequently I didn't make a fortune but what football did for me was to enable me to travel and I have been to some fantastic places, met some wonderful people from all walks of life and have a catalog of great memories.

It has been a fantastic journey and I have shed a few tears along the way, some of them tears of sadness over friends that are no longer with us, but mostly tears of laughter over the fun time I had playing this wonderful game!

My second book 40th Anniversary Socccr Bowl 77 Seattle Sounders Vs New York Cosmos is the result of a series of events that happened to me in a period of about six months...

September 2015 waiting for the results of my colonoscopy.

Saturday 26th September 2015 I had just received an email from Jenni Conner to say Congrats you are now an author. Within the space of 30 minutes I got a letter from the hospital to confirm that I have bowel cancer. (Talk about a roller coaster ride)

Tuesday 20th October 2015 the day of my surgery (Not pleasant)

Monday 14th December 2015 I start my rehab.

Tuesday 5th January 2016 I start back to work at the college (First hurdle)

Friday 27th May 2016 I officially retire from work although I am not 65 until November.

Monday 30th May 2016 I accept the position as Manager of Brightlingsea Regent U21 team

(Retirement short lived)

Friday 3rd June 2016 I lay in bed struggling to nod off, it didn't help that my wife Jo was snoring for England. We had not long been home after going out for a meal with the family.

Prior to going out I had been going through some old emails, one of which was from Adrian Hanauer the Seattle Sounders Majority Owner who I had written to in regards to my book Eternal Blue Forever Green and in it he says I was his mother's favorite player. I don't know whether it was this that started me thinking but as I lay there it kept running through my mind that if I had to rewrite the book I was sure I could do a much better job. I then started to think about the 77 Soccer Bowl team that I had played on and that next year it would be the 40th Anniversary of that wonderful game in Portland, against the New York Cosmos and the great Pele!

I knew I had to share this with Jenni Conner the publisher of Eternal Blue Forever Green so the next day

I called her to get her reaction and to see that if she liked the idea maybe we could put something together.

Again Jenni came through – book number two!

Book number three came about during my recent visit to Seattle when having lunch with Jenni and Bill Conner, Dave and Linda Gillett and Dave Butler. Jenni and I were talking about the two books and perhaps doing a compilation with a piece about returning to Seattle after an absence of 26 years. On returning from my visit and still buzzing I thought what a lovely way to bring my involvement with the Sounders to a close by making the final chapter about my visit and being awarded the Golden Scarf.

CHAPTER ONE
In the Beginning

As a young lad growing up in England, I supported my hometown club, Colchester United and I went along to all their home games with my dad and later on with my teammates from school. I was lucky because all of my friends loved to play football and we had a very good school team. I was first scouted playing for my school team and it was not long before I was selected for the

Colchester and District rep. team, which is when Colchester United first showed an interest in me.

John Chandler was a PE teacher at Wilson Marriage school in Colchester and was also the Colchester United Youth team Manager. At 12 years old I signed a schoolboy form and at 14 I started training with the Youth team who played in the Mercia League. I was the youngest one there and initially John took me along for the experience. At 15 I made my debut for the Youth team playing alongside the 3 apprentices at the club Dave Lamont, Richard Freeman and Peter Barlow. We beat Ipswich at Portman Road 1-0 and I got the assist. John did a great job recruiting all the better young players in the area and he did all he could to make sure that we were given every opportunity. At that time football was very big in the schools and there were a lot of great rivalries. There was no Sunday League Youth football then, so there was no age divisions as such – if you were good enough you played! Although I was not the biggest back then, I think playing with and against the older and bigger boys toughened me up.

John also use to do a bit of physio work for the club and often when we trained at Layer Road we would get to meet the pro's. I knew then that this is what I wanted to be, a professional footballer!

In the road where I lived was another young lad, Phil Day, who was was about 3 years older than me and was on the books at Ipswich Town. Phil was friendly with Colchester United brothers Ronnie and Bobby Hunt and during the offseason I would join them on their Sunday morning road run over to Tiptree to try to maintain a good fitness base. It would then be over to the park where Bobby would give us a lesson on how to finish. I was still only 15 when I made a half a dozen appearances for the reserve team in the London Midweek League and because I was still at school I had to get permission from Mr. Green our Headmaster. This was a football education in itself, playing alongside the likes of Reg Stratton, Peter Bullock, Ken Hodgson, Johnny Martin, John Mansfield and Roger Joslyn who were all first team players.

Ex Stoke and England legend Neil Franklin was the Manager and Scotsman John Anderson was his number two. I got to know them really well during my school holidays as I would partner Roger Joslyn and we would play them at head-tennis in the afternoons when they had finished working with the first team. In my 4th year of secondary school Neil offered me an apprenticeship but I was advised by my PE teacher Peter Hurst an ex pro and my dad to stay on the extra year at school to do my GCSE's. I decided to take their advice, Neil was great and reassured me that the offer would still be available when I had finished my exams. I continued to play for both the youth and reserve teams when it didn't interfere with my school work.

Before I joined Colchester United I turned down the chance to sign for our neighbours, Ipswich Town which was my mother's home town and where my grandparents still lived. They were in the old First Division and it was where Bobby Hunt was now playing. Reg Tyrell, was the youth team manager and was keen to sign me. I remember First Team Manager Bill McGarry and Bobby coming to our house to talk to my mum and dad about signing for the Town but I had already made up my mind that it was Colchester United and Neil Franklin that I wanted to play for. Just before I signed in 1968 Neil Franklin was sacked as the team were relegated but true to his word, he talked to the Board of Directors and on his recommendation they went ahead and signed me.

Although I was excited and couldn't wait to get started, I was disappointed Neil would not be there. I had supported the team for as long as I could remember, standing in the terraces as a schoolboy, watching the likes of Ames, Fowler, Forbes, Wright and King. I was also disappointed that my best mate from school Alan Dennis, was not offered an apprenticeship. We had played our very first school game together, played for the district and in our last year of school for the youth and reserve teams. Although we continued to play for the youth and reserves the big difference was while I was training full-time, Alan was doing a plumbing apprenticeship.

CHAPTER TWO
A Fork, a Wheelbarrow and a Paintbrush

During my first season I was the only apprentice and as if that was not hard enough they brought in Dick Graham as the new manager. The only consolation for me was that John Anderson remained as his number two.

I left school on a Friday in June 1968 and started at the club on the Monday. My first job was to assist the groundsman Geoff Gasson to get the pitch ready for the new season. After Geoff had finished telling me that Roger Joslyn had been the best apprentice he had help him (and I thought I was there to be a footballer) he handed me a fork and my first job was to remove all the plantain from the pitch and believe me there was much more of that than there was grass!

As I have always done when challenged, I tackled the task by saying to myself I was going to do it much quicker and better than Roger had done. I had no sooner finished that when my next job was to move God knows how many tons of sand and topsoil from the car park onto the pitch for Geoff to spread. My fork was replaced with a shovel and a wheelbarrow. When the pitch was done I was passed on to the maintenance guy, I think his name was Mac and my next job was to paint the two dressing rooms and the referees room, so he left me with several gallons of blue and white paint and a one inch paintbrush and I never saw Mac for another two weeks.

During this time, I hadn't met the new manager and it wasn't until everyone returned for pre-season training with John Anderson coming in a couple of days earlier, that it was explained what my role was and what to expect. Basically, my role was that I did all the chores and because I was the only apprentice, I would train with the pro's. My day started with getting the players training kit out and getting the equipment ready for training- balls, bibs and cones etc. If we did two sessions like in pre-season or whenever Dick got pissed off, I had to get it dry and have it ready for the afternoon session. At the end of the day, I had to mop both dressing room floors and on match days, get the players boots and match balls ready for the game. This often required re-lacing the balls and applying dubbin to them.

I thought the first month of working around the ground had been hard, but now I had to do all the chores and train. Dick came in for pre-season and on the very first day we did the Layer run, which brought us out at Friday Woods and back to the ground (it must have been 10 miles). When we got back to the ground while the pro's had their lunch break, I had to get the kit dried off ready for the afternoon session, while trying to find a bit of time to have lunch myself. The afternoon sessions were over at the Hilly Fields, which I knew well as I had represented my school in the district cross country there on several occasions. The big difference this time was that Dick had us doing interval runs up a hill with dumb bells in our hands. I will never forget that first day as when I got home I went straight up to bed and it was only my dad getting me up the next morning and kicking my arse that got me to go back!

That pre-season was an 8-5 job and to be honest it was pretty much that way during the season. Basically Dick came in and was very much a bully. He was your typical " drill sergeant major " and during my first season he got rid of top players such as Duncan Forbes and Derek Trevis and replaced them with players he had worked with at his other clubs. There was always a fear factor involved but what surprised me the most looking back was that someone didn't just knock him out!

My first season was very tough but with the help and support of John Anderson, Dennis Mochan and Roger Joslyn I survived. To be fair the players Dick brought in were great. They knew I was the only apprentice and looked out for me. There were some really good players and some great characters and the thing that got me through it was being able to train with experienced pro's like Bobby Cram, Brian Wood, Brian Gibbs and Terry Dyson as the coaching I received from Dick himself was minimal.

In my first season as an apprentice we played in the South Eastern Counties League playing against the likes of Chelsea, Arsenal, Tottenham, QPR, Fulham, Crystal Palace and Millwall, featuring young starlets such as Alan Hudson, Steve Perryman, Graeme Souness, Malcom MacDonald and Charlie George. I think we finished a very respectable fifth our first season.

I remember going to Tottenham early in the season and getting beat 13-1, I scored our goal and I remember coming off the pitch and getting a pat on the head from the late great Bill Nicholson. Later in the season we played them again in SECL Cup at Layer Road and beat them 2-1. The next day to my surprise Dick pulled me to one side and gave me a chitty to go and get a new pair of boots from Harpers sports shop in the town. Where we really gained our experience was playing in the reserves in the London Midweek League where Dick would play who he thought were his best young prospects with seasoned pros.

I would have to admit my relationship with Dick that

first season wasn't great and if I am honest it didn't really ever get much better! I was saddened when John Anderson got fed up with Dick's mood swings and left to be Jimmy Melia's number two at Aldershot. I remember one day we did a morning and afternoon session, so as usual, I had to get the kit dried off ready for the afternoon. In the boot room under the main stand at the ground, was a washing machine and on the floor was a long gas pipe that we would hang the kit over to dry it off. It looked a bit like a row of Bunsen Burners and you could adjust the height of the flames. On this particular day I didn't have a lot of time so I put it on full blast, thinking I would just sit there while it dried. I remember it was warm and snug in there and I must have dozed off. The next thing I remember was the kit was in flames! I quickly got everything under control but the kit was destroyed and the wooden stand above was all singed. I started to panic, knowing I would be in for a bollocking and possibly the sack when Dick returned. When he and the players returned he sorted out an alternative training kit and simply said to me " I will see you in the morning 9am sharp in my office " I don't think I slept that night and the next day I did get the bollocking, but it was for putting the fire out as he said the club would have been able to get a new stand from the insurance!

Overall I was pleased with my first season at the club, I was playing regular in both the youth team and reserves and had put in some good performances. I played up front in the youth team and was leading scorer and in the reserves either RB or RW. At this time we had five pro's that were all local guys and had gone to school in

Colchester, they were GK Alan Buck, Roger Joslyn, John Mansfield, Peter Barlow and Terry Price who I still remain good friends with today. These were all good players who again all came through John Chandler but unfortunately were all surplus to Dicks requirements. Although Terry was from Colchester he started his career with Leyton Orient and also played for England Youth. He was great with the younger players and I loved the times I played in the reserves when he was RW and Johnny Martin was LW. They had a very different style of play, Terry was very direct whereas Johnny would like to beat his man two or three times while giving him some verbal.

In my second season, through Dick's London based scout, John Kouhan, Micky Cook was brought in as an apprentice alongside me and was later followed by Keith Kilbourne, Steve Davis, Steve Foley, Phil Bloss, John McLaughlin and Lindsey Smith. I thought great, this will make my workload a bit easier but it never really did as they all traveled in on the train and would have to leave early meaning I got stuck mopping the dressing rooms. However having these guys training full time meant we worked together a lot more on the training ground and I think it definitely helped our team performances and it showed when we went over to Holland and won the big youth tournament there.

I knew my second season (1969-70) would determine whether or not I got a professional contract so I had to make sure I kept improving. Micky was about six months older than me so I thought it was a good sign when he got a pro contract. I started the season well scoring in both the youth and reserve games but it went a little tits up when we played Fulham's youth team over at the Garrison. We started the game really well and I put us 1-0 up in the first 10 mins. Shortly after that Dick showed up and started making changes. He told me to go and play out wide on the right, being young and a bit hot headed, I told him to F*** Off. With that, he pulls me off and I never played in the reserves midweek game or the youth game the following weekend. However I was back the following week and I remember playing WestHam in the FA Youth Cup where we lost 3-1. I also remember big Clyde Best scoring with a bullet header from outside the penalty area and the game being refereed by Peter Heard, who years later became the Chairman at the club. At the end of the season we played Millwall at Layer Road in the SECL Cup Final which we lost 2-1 and I scored our goal. I felt I had finished the season on a high and was quite confident I would get a pro contract.

As an apprentice in my final year I was on £10 a week so going pro I expected to be offered £16-19 plus the £250 signing on fee. However, and it came as no surprise when Dick offered me £16 a week but no signing on fee. It didn't seem to matter to him that I was the one who did the bulk of the chores as well as playing for the youth and reserve teams. I was absolutely gutted, however the only thing I really wanted to be able to say was that I was a professional footballer, so I accepted the offer. What really added salt to the wounds was when my good mate Alan Dennis, who had initially been told he wasn't as good a prospect as me, was offered £16 plus the signing on fee.

Although I was angry at Dick I was really pleased for Alan because we had played all our school football together and were now turning pro together.

I knew for me to get into the first team I either had to be playing out of my skin or Dick had to move on. The one consolation was I didn't have to do those chores any more and it felt good to know that when training was over I could go into town and have a coffee or lunch with the lads.

Unlike modern times, when the team sheet went up there would only be one substitute and for the away games, usually a 13th man. The first time I was 13th man for the first team I remember sitting on the coach traveling to Brentford in April 1970 and hoping one of the lads might get travel sickness so I would be elevated into the playing squad. The other reason I remember the game so well is that big Bobby Howlett broke his leg after coming on as a sub late in the game and afterwards the coach taking him to the hospital. After a lengthy period, he was allowed to travel back on the coach with us, grimacing in pain every time we went over a pot hole. Bobby was a big strong lad, a real " no nonsense centre back " and was a lovely lad off the field. But I don't think he was helped by Dick's rehab program, which involved him doing long road runs in army boots, which I think was imposed on him to soon and in the end, he had to retire from playing.

I was 13th man on a few more occasions but came to the conclusion that I was only really being taken along to help Denis Mochan with the kit and boot skips.

I really missed playing in the SECL it was a really good league and some quality players came out of it. My football development continued playing in the reserves and I enjoyed playing with the likes of first team players Jimmy Oliver, Brian Hall and Danny Light who played when out of favour with Dick. I remember one trip where the team coach got a flat tyre and before you could say Brian Hall (Henry or Busy as he was called) he was off the coach and changing the tyre. Trying to tighten the nuts the wheel kept turning so he asked Jimmy Oliver to put his foot on the brake. Jimmy was a bit of a joker himself and when he saw that Henry was at full strain he took his foot off the brake and Henry must have landed 50 yards up the road!

Another prankster was winger Terry Dyson the ex Tottenham player from the 1961 Double Winning team. I remember one evening game, Dick was giving his team talk in the dressing room with his back to the players writing something on the board. Terry got up from where he was sitting, crept up behind Dick and tapped him on his foot with his comb. Dick looked down and then up and carried on. Terry did it another two or three times and in the end Dick throws the chalk down and shouts at trainer Denis Mochan " Denis get that f*#&ing drip fixed!"

I guess the icing on the cake for me, came when I was selected to play in club secretary, Claude Orrin's testimonial game against Millwall. On the night I came up against Keith Weller, who was being looked at by several of the big clubs and I had a really good game. In the local newspaper the next day it said I had done really well. That weekend, club skipper Bobby Cram, who played right back, was injured and I thought this must be my big chance to break into the first team. How wrong could I be? Dick chose to play Micky Cook and the rest is history, for he would eventually go on to establish himself and set a club record number of appearances.

CHAPTER THREE
Playing Poker in the Southern League

I was devastated to be overlooked and knew it was time to move on from Colchester. Over the years of playing for the club, I had gotten to know Reg Tyrell, the former Ipswich Town youth team manager, really well. Reg was now the number two to John Bond (Kevin Bond's dad) at AFC Bournemouth, so I decided to give him a call to get some advice. He told me I should get my release and he would sort out a trial for me at Bournemouth. I made arrangements to talk to Dick Graham about getting my release. He invited me over to his house to discuss the situation, which went along the lines of, " I can't let you go to Bournemouth, because if you go there and do well, it wouldn't look good on me. " Before I could respond, he quickly followed up by saying he had however fixed me up at Hillingdon Borough FC, a leading Southern League club at the time, based in the West London suburbs. I told him I needed time to go away and think about it. I knew he couldn't just release me, but I knew if I stayed, he would make my life miserable. I got back on the phone to Reg, who advised me to go back to him and say I will go to Hillingdon if they pay me £19 a week, give me the £250 signing on fee and get me a full-time job.

This way, Bournemouth could continue to monitor my progress. The deal was done. They got me a job at Pyles Paints for another £19 a week and I moved into digs in West Drayton. I had gone from earning £16 a week, to £38 per week, plus £250 in the bank. Also my place of work and the football club were within walking distance of my digs.

Obviously, leaving Colchester was a big wrench for me. It was my hometown and all I had ever really wanted to do was to play first team football for them.

Hillingdon, in the Southern League, was not exactly what I had in mind, but my plan was to play out the season and go to Bournemouth the following season. Hillingdon turned out to be a frustrating time for me and at the end of the season, I was left thinking, at 19 years old, perhaps it was time to look outside the game.

After I arrived at Hillingdon, it was two weeks before I got a game. Although they were not doing great in the league, they were on a bit of a cup run which finally saw us reach the final of the FA Trophy against Telford and the ex-Wolverhampton legend, Ron Flowers, at the famous Wembley Stadium. What I didn't know at the time of my arrival, was that Dick had actually done the deal with the Chairman and that player-manager, Jim Langley the ex Fulham, QPR and England international, had no say in me going there. What a great start!

I decided to stick it out, as I was in lovely digs, the guys I worked with were good fun and I was making good money. I worked Monday to Friday and trained two nights a week and to be fair to Langley, he did give me playing time. He would play himself in the cup games and I would play the league games. He would play the home games and I would play the away games. This was very frustrating because it was hard for me to get any real consistency to my game. I remember playing in a midweek game before a cup game on the Saturday and one of the opposition players going over the top on me and needing to have five stitches in the gash on my shin. This meant I had to sit out the game on the Saturday thinking it was typical of my luck, as Jim slipped back into the team who won the game. On the upside, on the away trips, I learned to play poker and on a couple of occasions, I doubled my weekly wage!

The highlight of my short time at Hillingdon, was playing against WestHam at Lea Stadium in a friendly one evening and lining up against Harry Redknapp who later became my teammate and coach at Seattle and Trevor Brooking, who scored in a 1-1 draw. Although it was probably my best game, come Saturday, I was back on the bench.

The biggest disappointment was being named 13th man for the final at Wembley. Although I was involved in all the build-up and got all the bonuses, it just wasn't the same sitting on the bench as a mere spectator.

Jim started the game and to be fair, played very well, however, by halftime, the Wembley turf had taken its toll and his legs were gone as Telford went onto win the game 3-2. The disappointment was short-lived as we went back and partied at the clubhouse until the early hours of the morning.

After the relatively short spell at Hillingdon, I moved back home to Colchester, very disillusioned with the game. My mum and dad had always been very supportive of me playing football, but I took it on board when my mum said perhaps it was time to get a proper job. The one good thing about my time at Hillingdon, was that I came back with a few bob in my pocket, so I went out and bought a car and got a job working for the council.

I hadn't really given football to much thought, when I got an offer from former Colchester United wing-half John Docherty, who was manager at non-league Bury Town. So I started the 1971-72 season with them. To be honest, my heart wasn't really in it, but another former teammate and one of my best mates, Neil ' Twiggy '

Partner, who I had played with at Colchester United, persuaded me to join him over at Tiptree United. They were managed by another former teammate Roy Massey, who played CF for Colchester and Leyton Orient. Although I was a bit reluctant, it turned out to be just the tonic I needed, as I got my enthusiasm back and started to enjoy my football again.

Things took a dramatic turn for both Twiggy and I, when after a game late in the 1971-72 season, Roy pulled us to one side and told us that Colchester United skipper Bobby Cram, had been appointed player coach of the Vancouver Spartans in Canada and he wanted to take us over with him. Again, before I made my decision, I called Reg Tyrell who said that he thought it was a great opportunity and that I should go ahead and try my luck. He also said he thought it would be good to get my fitness level back up and when I got back he would arrange the trial. It sounded like a good plan as Bournemouth were just finishing their season, so when I got back the new season over here would be just underway and I would have a good fitness base. So after meeting up with Bobby Cram, two days after the season finished on May 5 1972, we flew out from Stansted Airport into Seattle – the city where I would ultimately settle for six seasons. After going through customs and immigration, we were driven up to the very impressive city of Vancouver BC.

CHAPTER FOUR
A Great Canadian Adventure

What a wonderful adventure it was to be, pitching up in Canada, four young guys like us!

However, in the back of my mind, was a plan to give it a go for the season and then return to the UK where I would take up Reg Tyrell's offer of a trial with AFC Bournemouth.

I was now 20 and it had always been my dream to be a professional footballer. This ambition dominated all of my thinking. My three and a half years at Colchester United had been a good grounding, but time was now ticking on. I remained convinced that in the right environment, I could still make a living playing football. I thought what a bonus having Bobby Cram as player-coach, he had played for the Spartans and knew the area well. I would go on to play two seasons for them in a semi-professional league in BC. In my second season because it was still only part time I got a job working for RCA Ltd. in there warehouse.

Although I was enjoying life in Vancouver, playing for the Spartans did not provide the full time football environment I was looking for. The break I was looking for came when it was announced that Vancouver had been awarded a franchise in the North American Soccer League (NASL) and I was invited to train with a select group of players that they were interested in signing. It was revealed the new set-up would be called the Vancouver Whitecaps, but rather disappointingly, they would only be part-time their first season. Again not what I was looking for! The disappointment soon turned to joy however, when after playing for the Spartans in the BC League Cup Final which we won and I happened to have a very good game. Unbeknown to me, John Best, the newly appointed manager of the Seattle Sounders, another new NASL franchise was watching the game and after our celebrations he approached me and offered me a contract. Seattle was just down the highway from Vancouver and John assured me that they would be full-time and that Jimmy Gabriel, the ex Everton, Southampton and Scottish International, was going to be his player/assistant coach. I was quickly sold on what John had to say and didn't hesitate to accept the offer. Yes! I was back in the pro game!

By then I was almost 23, was married to my first wife Patricia and had a young son Jason. It was such a big relief to get this break, it felt like everything I had worked so hard for was now beginning to fall into place and this was my chance to show that given the opportunity, I could play at the pro level. As you will read, I went onto spend six seasons with the Sounders and of course life there was full of highs and lows but looking back after all these years it was, without doubt, the best experience of my life. To play for such a fantastic club, in such a beautiful city, in front of those incredible fans and to make some lifelong friends, was truly a privilege and I am proud to be a part of the Sounders history.

I think John Best had come to the Final in Vancouver to take a look at a number of young Canadian players that were starting to make a bit of a name for themselves, but at the end of the game it was the former WBA and Colchester skipper Bobby Cram, Phil Trenter and myself that were offered contracts with the Sounders. My good mate Twiggy decided to return to England.

Although excited and looking forward to the new challenge, I was still a bit apprehensive about it all and wondered if I had made the right decision. Although I had done well in the two seasons I played for the Spartans, I couldn't help but think back to my start with them where I got five yellow cards in my first six games, which lead to a six weeks suspension. I was coming from a semi-pro league where I also held down a full-time job and now had a wife and young son to support. I knew going into full time training would not be a problem, as I had always kept myself in good shape, but the thing that caused me most anxiety was not wanting it to go wrong and letting my family down as we had been planning our future in Vancouver.

CHAPTER FIVE
The Inaugural Season 1974

1974 Seattle Sounders

(Back Row, L-R) Walt Daggatt - Managing General Partner, Willie Penman, Hank Liotart, Tjeert Van't Land, Dave Landry, Barry Watling, Ballan Campeau, Roger Goldingay, Dave Gillett, John Rowlands, Pepe Fernandez, Jack Daley - General Manager.

(Front Row, L-R) Hal Childs - Public Relations Director, Roy Sinclair, Adrian Webster, Dave Butler, Jack Curran - Trainer, John Best - Head Coach, Jim Gabriel, Bernie Fagan, Alan Stephens, David D'Errico, Otey Cannon.

Prior to moving to Seattle, I had only been there on one other occasion and that was in the summer of 72 when Bobby Cram took me and a couple of my Spartans teammates to watch Aberdeen Vs Wolverhampton Wanderers in an Exhibition game at Memorial Stadium and then onto the after party. Who would have thought two years later 1 would be playing for the Seattle Sounders in the same stadium.

We moved into an apartment on Queen Anne Hill close to Memorial Stadium where we would train and play our games. The apartments were quite basic but served the purpose through the first season.

The makeup of the team was a mixture of English, Scottish, Dutch and young American players, a nice balance of youth and experience and the pre-season was all about getting to know your teammates. Right from the start, it was evident that the management team of Daley, Best and Gabriel wanted to create a family type environment that would soon open up to include the fans that packed the stadium.

The pre-season went well and I had done enough to win a starting place in the lineup for the opening game of the season away to the LA Aztecs. Unfortunately, we lost the game 2-1 and although I didn't have a great game playing in midfield, I didn't think I was any better or worse than one or two of the others. However, my worse fears became reality when I was the one who was dropped to the bench for the home opener against the Denver Dynamo. It was a sell-out crowd and the lads played really well and went onto win 4-0. I had mixed emotions as I was pleased for the team but knew it might be a while before I would get another chance.

The one thing I had learned from my Vancouver experience where I got five yellow cards in my first six games and a six weeks suspension was that I was just going to have to take it on the chin, get my head down, work even harder and hope my chance would come sooner than later.

My chance came eight games into the season when my teammate and former Spartans coach Bobby Cram who had also signed for the Sounders was unable to make training and therefore was not considered for the next game which also lead to his departure. I was sorry to see Bobby go, he had given me my opportunity to play in Canada and how ironic should it be that the next game was against the Vancouver Whitecaps, the team I had turned down to join the Sounders.

Fate had stepped in again and I traveled up to Vancouver knowing I would be playing against many of the players I had played with and against during my time there. I don't really remember to much about the game only that John had asked me to play RB and I would come up against my old rival Sergio Zanatta who was not only a good player but was a bit of a wind up merchant as well. During the game, I had to keep reminding myself not to react or do anything silly that might get me sent off. We won the game 2-0 and I remember coming off the field a much happier player than I did in my first game in LA and it felt really good when John pulled me to one side to say well done and then to go on to meet up with my family was very special! I must have done ok, for I went onto play the rest of the season at RB and I continued in that position for another two seasons.

When I think about the Best and Gabriel partnership, it was quite amazing how they developed such a good working relationship knowing they were cross town rivals when John was at Liverpool and Jimmy at Everton. I guess the common denominator was that they both loved their football and both wanted us to try to play it the right way. Because Jimmy was still playing, he was that bit closer to the players whereas John was able to take a step back and make those important decisions that one has to make.

I loved the training sessions and for the first time, I felt I was getting some quality coaching. We did a lot of Shadow play, working on good team shape and balance and getting a better understanding of our individual roles. On match days John would deliver the team talk, he was very meticulous and the emphasis would always be on winning your individual battles. He felt that if you had 7 players on top of their own game, you always had a chance of winning, also knowing that on the day one or two might have an off day. Playing at the stadium and to a full house created a tremendous atmosphere and it became our fortress and the bond between the players and fans was incredible, something I had never experienced before.

Quite often after training, we would all go over to the Pancake House for lunch where we soon got to know all the staff and the regulars. It was much the same after our home games, we would all meet up with the fans at the after party, sign some autographs and have a beer or two with them. It was incredible how well received we were by the fans who came from all walks of life. It was like they just couldn't do enough for you and there generosity and hospitality extended to include the players wives, girlfriends and siblings.

As I said earlier after the opening game of the season against LA , I was a little low, so I decided I would just get my head down and work my socks off to try to get back into the team.

It was the third game of the season when the team lost Pepe Fernandez with a broken leg. This was a big blow for the team, but for me, it turned out to be just the tonic I needed, as whenever Pepe came along to our training sessions he always gave me lots of encouragement and advice. He would say to me you are a good defender so just play to your strengths.

ADRIAN WEBSTER

THE PLAYERS

PEPE FERNANDEZ

A forward, Pepe joined the NASL in 1967 coming from his native Uruguay to play for the Los Angeles Toros. When John signed him for the Sounders, he quickly became the fans favourite son. Pepe is one of the most charismatic people I have ever met. He was like a magnet, people were just drawn to him and he made time for everyone.

At the start of our second season Dave Gillett, Pepe and I went over to Spokane to promote a pre-season game that we were scheduled to play there. On the flight home on a 10-12 seater plane, it became a bit of a bumpy ride. Dave and I sat opposite each other and Pepe sat behind us. Suddenly the plane tipped to one side and Dave and I watched as the pilot struggled to straighten it up. We both turned to see how Pepe was doing and we're almost scared out of our seats as the usual jovial Pepe had turned ash grey.

Another place Pepe showed what a great entertainer he was would be at the various club functions where he would get out his guitar and serenade everyone.

I often think when I am watching the Premier League games over here in England what would Pepe be worth today with his silky skills. He had the ability to go by players just like George Best, he was brave, good in the air and scored goals.

Unfortunately, although he did get back playing again, he was never quite the same player, but to us and his fans, he was the Sounders Pele!

BIG JOHN

Another larger than life character was big John Rowland's a rugged good looking guy with a boxers shaped nose that looked like he had gone a few rounds. Before coming to the US John had applied his trade in the lower divisions of the English Football League. At 6' 1" he was a big strong in your face centre-forward who backed down from no one. He was good in the air, could hold the ball up for you and he scored goals but what he did best was intimidate the opposition. The number of times I had a little chuckle to myself after he had just nailed someone, he would just jog off and as he passed you by give you a cheeky little wink.

He certainly knew how to push my buttons for as many times as I would react to a situation he would just grab me by the scruff of the neck pull me in and just give me a big old smile.

John played two seasons for the Sounders scoring 19 goals in 41 appearances before moving to the San Jose Earth Quakes.The camaraderie between the players that first season was something special and each player brought something different to the makeup of the team.

Roy Sinclair who took so much stick but would just bounce back hence the nickname Rubber Roy or Dave Butler who didn't let a day go by without telling a joke and then laugh louder than anyone else. Great Team Spirit!

Although it was a great first season and we finished with a W13 L7 record, we did not qualify for the playoffs. We had come up a little short however what I think it did do was to build a strong foundation for the following season.

Our last game of the season was against the Vancouver Whitecaps at home and what made it special was that the management team thought it would be a nice gesture for the players to go into the crowd and hand out flowers to show our appreciation for their tremendous support throughout the season. (Thankfully there were several attractive ladies in the crowd) It was also very special for me because we did the double over them winning the game 2-1 with goals from Gabriel and Rowland's and it just reinforced that I had made the right decision.

THE OFF SEASON

At the end of the season, I had a decision to make, whether to return to Vancouver or to stay in Seattle as it was only a seasonal contract and I would have no money coming in. I was told by John that they wanted me back for the next season so I went to see General Manager Jack Daley who said he would get me a job at Nordstrom's so we decided to stay.

I tell the story of my experience at Nordstrom's in my first book Eternal Blue Forever Green. It didn't quite go to plan (thank God) because I was offered several coaching opportunities in the area.

My contract for the 74 season was $800 a month plus an apartment. I was now picking up $500 a week coaching at various clubs in the area. I thought I had won the lottery!

During the season when we went on the road trips I never seemed to have as much money in my pockets as some of the other guys, so I decided with my new found wealth and once I had taken care of my family needs I would stick the rest away to cover any short falls there might be next season. Instead of putting it into a bank account I put it under the spare wheel in my car, so I had easy access to it. No I didn't have my car stolen! However one day we decided to go up to Vancouver to visit the family. On the way up we get a blowout, so I get out of the car and walk around to the trunk to get the spare out. Feeling really pissed off because not only have I got to change the tyre it is also blowing a gale. Just as I lift the spare, Pat my wife at the time walks around and sees all this money laying there. All I could think of to say was (as we hadn't long had the car) it must have been a druggies!

To rub salt into the wounds when we got back from Vancouver Pat went out and brought all these new pots and pans. Moral of the story was I should have stuck it in the bank at least I would have got some interest.

With the rest of the money and the bit of savings we had, we took a trip back to England to visit my family and during the couple of months we were there I trained and played with one of the non-league clubs to stay in shape!

1975 SEASON

1975 Seattle Sounders

(Back Row, L-R) Walt Daggatt - Managing General Partner, David D'Errico, Hank Liotart, Dave Gillett, Mike England, Paul Gizzi, Barry Watling, Tjeert Van't Land, John Rowlands, Tim Logush, Pepe Fernandez, Jack Daley - General Manager.

(Front Row, L-R) Tim Haag - Public Relations Director, Arfon Griffiths, Manny Matos, Dave Butler, Frank Furtado - Trainer, John Best - Head Coach, Jim Gabriel, Alan Stephens, Tommy Baldwin, Paul Crossley, Adrian Webster.
40

It was sad to see the likes of Willie Penman, Roy Sinclair, Bernie Fagan and Otey Cannon not return but in came Paul Crossley from Tranmere Rovers, Arfon Griffiths the Wrexham and Wales International, Tommy Baldwin ex- Chelsea and perhaps the biggest name of all Mike England of Tottenham Hotspur's and Wales fame.

Training was still at Memorial Stadium and the introduction of the new guys saw the standard go up another notch.

Jack Curran who was our trainer in 74 had retired, he was a terrific guy who took no crap and the guys loved him. He was replaced by Frank Furtado, another super guy who doubled as trainer for the Seattle Super Sonics his first season. Both Jack and Frank were responsible for getting the guys interested in basketball and it was always a race to see who could get to them first for their comp tickets.

The family unity continued as several of the players and their families moved into an apartment complex over in Lynnwood. I think this also helped the new players coming over with their families to settle in quicker as it can be quite daunting when going to another country and meeting new people for the first time.

Around the pool in the afternoons became the hive of social activity where the wives bonded and the kids made new friends.

I remember one afternoon we were all gathered around the pool when Mike England made an appearance with his family. Mike and his wife Gwen were perhaps a little bit more upper class and were more likely to socialize away from the group. This particular afternoon it was extremely hot and the kids were in and out of the pool. From the other side of the pool, we watched as Gwen got up to go for a dip. At this time Alan Stephens two boys (who were a bit boisterous) and a few of the residents were having a swim. As Gwen headed off in the direction of the two boys and as she got closer to them she lets out the loudest scream at which point everyone jumped up and ran over to see what all the fuss was. On our arrival, everyone broke into hysterics when they saw floating on top of the pool a number two that one of the boys had done.

After losing the opening game of the season away to Vancouver, we won our next four games. GK Barry Watling was back for his second season and the partnership of Gillett and England looked formidable as Alan Stephens and I made up the back four. Griffiths and Baldwin showed their classes in the middle of the park while Tjeert Van't Land and Paul Crossley provided the pace on the flanks with Dave Butler linking up well with John Rowland's up front.

There were a few rivalries that carried over from the first season notably the one with the San Jose Earth Quakes who had the Demling brothers who thought the object of the game was to just kick the opposition. I'm glad we had Big John on our side and when Jimmy Gabriel played he didn't take to many prisoners either. I particularly enjoyed the games against Vancouver even though I took a bit of stick when we played up there!

A new rivalry would emerge as the Portland Timbers were awarded a new franchise making it five teams in the NASL Western Division.

I recently read the 1975 Portland Timbers book in which the author Michael Orr praises the support that Sounders Walt Daggatt gave them when coming into the league and how the Sounders were very much the role model when putting all the pieces together. They appointed an English coach, had a very strong British squad and got very much involved in the community.

The rivalry is still very strong today with both teams playing in the MLS.

1975 was perhaps the start of the big names coming over and there was no bigger name than that of Pele the Brazilian Superstar who signed for the New York Cosmos.

Our home game against the Cosmos was shortly after he had signed for them and was televised nationwide. It would be the first time the American public would get to see his silky skills.

In front of a sellout crowd, we won the game 2-0 with goals from Liotart and Baldwin. Danny Blanchflower the former Tottenham Hotspur captain was the colour commentator for the game. It was a tremendous atmosphere and I remember Pele getting a little frustrated as he went through wave after wave of tackles from Gillett and England. I think I might have got one or two in myself. It was my first time of playing against the great man and I still have a lovely photo with him and Barry Watling taken in the dressing room after the game. It was a mid-day KO and after the game, we partied with the fans who were in top form and I can't remember having to buy a beer.

Not only was Pele a great player he was also a great ambassador for the NASL and soccer in the US as attendances soared wherever he played.

I think the formula for the first couple of seasons was to bring in young players like Dave Gillett, Dave Butler and myself, players that were hungry and wanted to do well and to mix them with older more experienced players like Jimmy Gabriel, Willie Penman and Mike England.

The first two seasons of training and playing our games at Memorial Stadium were filled with much fun and laughter, as well as a work ethic that John and Jimmy believed would produce a winning and entertaining team. I loved the training almost as much as playing the games and the camaraderie in the team was brilliant!

Playing at Memorial Stadium to a full house, created a tremendous atmosphere and it became our 'fortress' the bond between the players and fans was magical!

We finished the season with a W15 L7 record that saw us into the playoffs. As we finished second in our division behind the Timbers meant we had to travel to Portland for the playoff game. We had split the regular seasons games, we won 1-0 at home with a goal from Jimmy Gabriel and lost 2-1 in Portland with Dave Gillett notching our goal.

On a personal note, I was gutted when John rested me the last game of the season to be ready for the playoff game and to give Manny Matos a run out as I had played every minute of every game.

I remember the playoff game in front of 32,523 being very physical and having a confrontation with Peter Withe after he made a sliding tackle with his cleats raised, so I ended up using him as a plank as I left a trail of my cleats along his body. In a very tight game we finally went down 2-1 in OT and at the end of the game, their fans bombarded the pitch. As they celebrated their victory, I remember making a couple of mental notes of one or two of their players that had rubbed me the wrong way for the following season.

The Timbers went onto reach the final eventually losing 2-0 to the Tampa Bay Rowdies in San Jose. I think Walt may have given them to much information!

MOVING STADIUMS

Moving from Memorial Stadium to the Kingdome in 1976 although it was a sad occasion it showed that the Sounders were moving in the right direction and were now able to accommodate the thousands of fans that previously had not been able to get a ticket.

The NASL was increasing in numbers and the move to the Kingdome was a part of the vision that the Managing General Partner, Walt Daggatt and General

Manager Jack Daley had for the club. They wanted the Sounders to be a model franchise and for the players to become household names.

We were now able to attract big clubs like Rangers from Scotland and Chelsea to come over and it showed that soccer was on the up in the US.

Memorial Stadium had become the Sunshine Stadium for us because during the time we played our games there I can't ever remember it raining and I don't think we lost to many games there either. We had so many fantastic times there, training, playing and bonding with the fans but to accommodate the thousands of fans who could not get a ticket for the game I think it was the right time to move on.

I can remember a couple of funny stories from our training sessions at Memorial Stadium, the first was about an Egyptian guy who rolls up pitch side in a white limousine and matching tracksuit with his agent who persuades John and Jimmy to give him a tryout. I tell the story in my book Eternal Blue Forever Green and the other was an American Indian who also gets John and Jimmy to let him tryout. Anyways he plays up front and every time he made a run to receive the ball he lets out the loudest war-like cry. After several of these runs Harry Redknapp who is refereeing the game is starting to get really annoyed and is just about to bring his trial to an end when one of the lads plays a lovely lofted pass into his path and as the ball drops over his shoulder he volleys it into the top corner of the goal. With this, he takes off on his celebration run making an even louder war-cry but what is even funnier is Harry takes off after him to join in the celebration. The guys are just cracking up, it was hilarious! However it was not enough to earn him a contract.

The Kingdome was a wonderful stadium and we were the first pro team to play there. In front of a crowd of 58,000 we played against the New York Cosmos lead by Pele who on the night put on a clinic as they went on to win 3-1.

Looking back I find it quite sad that the Kingdome is no longer standing. I'm sure it held a lot of wonderful memories for the thousands of fans that enjoyed watching the Sounders and the other Major League teams in the city that also played their games there.

1976 SEASON

I was really looking forward to the new season the incentive to do well was two-fold

1.To get to the Soccer Bowl Final as it was going to be played in the Kingdome.

2.To make sure that if we got there, I was in the team.

Again we said goodbye to players that had served the club well GK Barry Watling, D. Alan Stephens, M. Pacey Tjeert Van't Land and the quality of M. Arfon Griffiths and M. Tommy Baldwin.

In came the youthful GK. Tony Chursky, D. John Mc Laughlin M. Tommy Jenkins, M. Eric Skeels, M.

Jimmy Robertson, M. Harry Redknapp, F. Boris Bandov, F. Gordon Wallace, F. Geoff Hurst World Cup Winner and the only player to score a hatrick in the final plus GK. Mike Ivanow.

John had assembled a cast that he thought would grace the new stadium and hopefully take us to the Soccer Bowl Final.

Renton Stadium became our training ground and we would train at the Kingdome on the day before the game and the morning of the game, where we would do a warmup, go through our set pieces and finish with a scrimmage. Although the faces of my teammates had changed, the banter was still the same and the dressing room was still the place where you learned so much more about the character of your teammates.

The pressure for me to do well was enormous as each season John and Jimmy looked to improve the squad. As well as the young American players that had been drafted, players like Dave D'Errico, Manny Matos and Tim Logush young local players like Jimmy McAlister and Darrell Oak were starting to break into the system.

In training we finished most sessions with an 8 V 8 across the pitch using full size goals. Normally the shape of both teams would be a 2-3-2 giving you 2 diamonds creating width and depth as well as good shape and balance. The first team GK would play in one goal and the reserve GK in the other goal. The two CB's normally started with the first team GK and the two FB's with the reserve GK (the CB's would rotate with the FB's) a combination of 3 midfield players and

2 Forwards. What this did was get players playing as a partnership e.g.

Gillett and England or a unit e.g. Jenkins, Webster and Buttle, it also created lots of 1 V 1 battles as well as test the partnership of Hurst and Wallace up against Gillett and England. When we needed to develop our wing play, channels were added on either side and our wingers would work the channels to provide crosses. FB's were also added into the channels to work on support and overlaps.

Looking back over the season I would have to say it was very much a hit and miss season as we finished with a W14 L10 record. After losing our first game of the season 2-0 in St. Louis we won our next 3, we then lost 5 consecutive games and finished the season winning 6 out of the last 7.

I think we certainly had the class and flair in the team to do well but what I think was missing was that bit of steel Jimmy Gabriel gave us in midfield as he only played in 10 of our 24 league games.

On a personal note I was really pleased with my performance throughout the season and I was the only player to play every minute of every game. I also scored my first goal for the Sounders in the Kingdome winning 3-1 against the Minnesota Kicks. I arrived late in the box to get on the end of a poor clearance and to smash it into the roof of the net. Whilst doing so I think I wiped out one of their players so during the break in the action they kept showing it (the goal) on the big screen in the stadium. I still to this day don't know if the camera man was really pleased for me or was just taking the piss as I didn't score too many!

The most notable names from the 76 squad were Geoff Hurst, Jimmy Robertson and Harry Redknapp but the player that ticked all the boxes for me was...

GORDON WALLACE

Gordon was a native of Dundee who was a prolific goal scorer in the Scottish League. He was the perfect partner for Geoff Hurst up front and in his first season he scored 12 goals.

Unfortunately, he was unable to come back the following season but returned for the 78 season scoring 8 goals. He was a really nice guy who had a dry sense of humour and took his football very seriously. A really good pro! Not only was he very consistent but he also helped the younger less experienced players whereas Sir Geoff concentrated more on his own performance.

Our first season in the Kingdome we averaged 25,000 but unlike the very first crowds at Memorial Stadium the fans were now a bit more knowledgeable about the game (and a bit more critical) I remember in one of the early games at Memorial Stadium heading the ball clear from the edge of the 18 yard box to the halfway line and half the fans in the stand on that side of the field stood up and cheered. The players now had their own little cheering sections in different parts of the stadium Tony had " Chursky's Chics " and I had " Webster's Women ".

After the games we would head up to the lounge in the stadium where we would catch up with family, friends and fans. From there it would be on to a party or a nightclub where we were starting to become part of the Seattle social scene.

Another place we would hangout was Long Acres which was close to the training ground and where Harry would put his plan into action which was for us to follow who he thought were the big punters and to see who they were betting on and then we would place our bets.

During the season Pat and I got divorced, I think if I am honest the 3 seasons of giving myself to the Sounders and being back in the pro environment put a bit of a strain on our relationship. I think being a pro can make you a bit selfish, but I felt that I needed to give it my all if I wanted to stay in the game. The Sounders were very supportive of both Pat and I and she moved back to Vancouver with our two young children.

Our last game of the season was away to Vancouver where we went down 3-2. Five days later back in the Kingdome we played them in the playoffs and in front of 30,000 we won 1-0 with a goal from World Cup hero Geoff Hurst. In the next round we traveled to Minnesota where in front of 41,000 we lost 3-0.

There were a sprinkling of Sounders fans that had traveled to the game and were staying at the same hotel that ended up entertaining a few of the boys when we got back to the hotel.

As I said earlier the Final was to be played in Seattle so we were all very disappointed not to make it, however we all thought Minnesota deserved there place in the final when they beat San Jose 3-1.

In the final they lost 3-0 to Toronto and the Great Eusebio in front of 25,000 and as I sat there watching the game with my teammates I couldn't help but think had it been us out there playing the place would be packed (60,000)

As I watched Eusebio score from one of his spectacular free kicks my mind wandered back to the 66 World Cup when Pele was literally booted out of the tournament and Eusebio went onto win the Golden Boot and receive the accolades that Pele had as a young player in previous tournaments. Eusebio had done it again! As they did there lap of honour around the Dome little did I know that a year later we would be playing in the final against the ever improving New York Cosmos and my idol Pele. I just wished our final could have been in Seattle!

This was John's last season as Head Coach as he moved on to become General Manager of the Vancouver Whitecaps.

JOHN BEST

The first 3 seasons with the Sounders were absolutely brilliant and the part John played, along with Walt Daggatt, Jack Daley and Jimmy Gabriel in the teams success was enormous.

John had begun his career in England with Liverpool and Tranmere Rovers, but it was in the US where he established himself as a top Player, Coach and General Manager. Prior to joining the Sounders as Head Coach he played for the Dallas Tornado and spent six seasons in the NASL where he was a five-time first team All-

Star and in 1973 he earned a cap playing for the US National team.

From the first day I arrived in Seattle John was the one person I could talk to and come away thinking I was a much better player than I actually was. As a player I got to see all of John's many qualities: his good looks, his charm, man management skills, dignity, humour... I could go on. Not only was he a very good coach he was very good at promoting the game and it almost felt like he was being groomed to be a General Manager and sure enough he later would leave the Sounders to take up the GM position with the Vancouver Whitecaps. Over his 3 seasons as Coach, he compiled a W43 L26 record.

I believe Daley, Best and Gabriel helped to lay a strong foundation for pro soccer in the state of Washington and it is reflected in today's current MLS Sounders who lead the way in attendances averaging 40,000 a game.

I was saddened in 2014 to hear of the passing of John at a time when the Sounders were celebrating their 40th Anniversary. Coming from England myself, I know that if Coach Best had accomplished what he had in North America in the UK they would either erect a statue or name a stand after him.

To be the first Coach can never be emulated and I just hope one day his legacy will be recognized in a very special way.

PLAYING IN THE NASL

One of the things I enjoyed most about playing in the NASL was the traveling. We would fly out to most of the games and sometimes we would be on the road for up to 5 days. We got to see some beautiful cities, stayed in some top hotels and were generally well looked after. The first season we would just sign for our meals except for the pre-match meal which we all had together. This was normally steak, scrambled eggs and toast but because I think we abused the club's generosity when ordering breakfast and dinner by ordering the most expensive things on the menu, plus adding our bar bill to the tab, the following season the club gave us a daily per diem which I think was about $35 a day. Unfortunately, with the per diem a few of the lads used it to play poker which was another great past-time on the road trips and some of the Kitty's got to be quite high. We would play on the plane and continue it in one of the hotel rooms or out by the pool.

I remember Wayne Cody who covered our games, as well as being a big fan loved to join in the card school. Others in the media who occasionally traveled with us were Bob Robertson, Bruce King, Gordy Holt from the Seattle Post Intelligencer and Walt Parietti from the Seattle Times and like Wayne they were all good guys who I think genuinely enjoyed being around the lads!

Above all it was great traveling to all the different cities and when the club knew we were going to be there for a few days, they would organize a bit of sightseeing for us. Like a few of the other lads who had played in the lower divisions in England to now get the chance to play in some of these fabulous stadiums was just mind boggling and it gave you a bit of a lift when you ran out to play the game. Another thing that gave me a lift and made the hair on the back of my neck stand up was when they played the American National Anthem, I don't know why but it just did. No more so than when Lou Rawls sang it at one of our home games.

It didn't matter what city you played in you would

always come across players you knew or knew of and it didn't matter how the battle on the field had gone there was always an after party to go to. The worst thing about the after parties was that you were often on the road early next morning and usually nursing a sore head, but that didn't stop the card school from carrying on.

HEAD COACH: JIMMY GABRIEL

Jimmy Gabriel took over the reins in 1977 and all the players were over the moon when he was appointed Head Coach, as it made sense to try to maintain that continuity. Jimmy brought in Bobby Howe who he knew from his playing days with Bournemouth and introduced a reserve team which he left to the guidance of Harry Redknapp.

On the playing front he brought in Steve Buttle, Micky Cave, Mel Machin, Jocky Scott and Roger Cross who played eight games before getting injured and returning to England.

Jimmy joined the Sounders in its inaugural season as player/assistant coach. He was a tough rugged defensive midfielder who started his career with Dundee in Scotland and went on to have an illustrious career playing in England for Everton and Southampton and was capped twice for Scotland.

The first 3 seasons playing under John and Jimmy were amazing and Jimmy is one of the big reasons I signed for the Sounders as I thought what better player was there to help improve my game.

My first memory of Jimmy was him playing for Everton in the 1966 FA Cup Final against Sheffield Wednesday at the old Wembley. It was back in the days of black and white TV and I remember watching the game with one of my best mates who just happened to be a big Wednesday fan. So as you do, I chose to support Everton on the day, who went on to win 3-2 after falling behind by 2 goals.

As a player, you would rather have him on your team than play against you. He had a tremendous inner strength and I can remember him coming off the bench on a couple of occasions and turning the game around when it looked lost.

Jimmy had always been that bit closer to the players than John and I remember him once saying to me " I like to try to treat people how I would like to be treated " He had great man management skills and knew how to get the best out of his players. He made me the team captain and moved me back into midfield, this helped my confidence tremendously and I would have run through a brick wall for him. He is still the one person I have the upmost respect for. He was a very good player and coach and a very honest and caring person. Although we didn't get off to the best start in 77 he didn't panic, he simply made a couple of adjustments, brought in Tommy Ord and took us to the final. He instilled a belief in the players that we were good enough to go out and compete against the best.

Jimmy was another one who had hollow legs and could drink for Scotland (and England)

Whenever it was him and the lads around the table the beer mats, bottle tops and ashtrays were used to make a coaching point. We were on a road trip – I think it was Fort Lauderdale and we had a bit of down time, so we decided we would have a bit of a session at the pool. You have to keep in mind this was the mid – 70's and having a beer went hand in glove with playing! On this particular trip, Gordy Holt from the Seattle Post Intelligencer, had traveled with us and during the session, he made a remark that he didn't think it was very professional to consume the amount we had done. So the following day, Jimmy put us through our paces while Gordy just watched in amazement at the effort that was put into the training session.

Gabriel had done it again! Been there, done it got the T-Shirt!

I can't ever remember hearing anyone say a bad word about him – apart from when they were on the end of one of his crunching tackles.

BOBBY HOWE

Bobby started his career at WestHam and finished his playing days at Bournemouth. He joined up with Jimmy and Harry for the 77 season and played in the first few games of the season before slotting back into his coaching role.

His attention to detail was top drawer and I think his success as a coach with the Sounders can be measured by the fact he worked under Gabriel, Hinton and Calloway.

Bobby stayed in the Seattle area and was Coach of the US Men's U20 team at the 1993 World Youth Championship and later went onto become Coach of the Portland Timbers. He was also in charge of Education for Coaches for the US Soccer Federation.

His contribution to the pro game and youth soccer both in Washington State and the US has been enormous.

I was fortunate several years later to do my B License under him and I learned so much more about the game. After the course we had a couple of nights out and had a few good laughs. He also gave me a bit of coaching work before I went back to Phoenix to start my own coaching career.

ADRIAN WEBSTER

HARRY REDKNAPP

Harry started his career with WestHam where he played alongside the likes of World Cup winners Moore, Hurst and Peters. Before joining the Sounders in 76 he played with Jimmy Gabriel and Bobby Howe at Bournemouth managed by John Bond.

The three had always said that if the opportunity came up they would like to work together. Initially Harry came over to play but the constant training and playing on the AstroTurf took its toll so when Jimmy took over from John he made him one of his assistants. Both Harry and Bobby played the first game of the 77 season in Hawaii. Although Bobby worked more alongside Jimmy Harry would often step in when Jimmy was required elsewhere. His sessions always had that element of fun about them and always involved the ball.

Jimmy decided that he wanted to introduce a reserve team and this became Harry's role to develop the young American and Canadian players coming into the system and to work with Jimmy Johnston the Sounders Head Scout to identify the best young local talent.

The reserve team also gave the first team players somewhere to play when returning from an injury or

78

not getting a regular first team game. Harry did a great job of preparing these young players to make that step up to the first team and under his guidance players like Jimmy McAlister, Jeff Stock, Mark Peterson, Bernie James, Eddie Krueger and Ian Bridge all went on to have successful careers.

I thought Jimmy, Bobby and Harry were a good team and that their individual strengths complimented each other and it created a fun learning environment to work in. I think coaching for the Sounders gave Harry a great platform to build on and he went onto be a very successful manager in England and at one time was the favourite to get the vacant England job.

1977 SEASON

At the end of the 76 season John moved up to Vancouver and Dave Gillett, Manny Matos and myself rented his house over on Magnolia Drive.

After a short break, we were back into doing the promotional work, going into schools, doing soccer clinics, shopping mall appearances as well as guest speakers at Rotary clubs and other club functions, which helped season ticket sales and for us to become household names.

VEGAS

Before the season kicked off courtesy of Big Mike Ivanow, we had a long weekend in Vegas where we let our hair down before we started the serious business of pre-season training.

As far as we knew Mike had received a large bonus from the credit union his father had built up and he had booked three suites at Caesars Palace along with a bit of spending money.

Mike was not only large in stature he was a big character who certainly enjoyed the good life and was very generous to his teammates.

On arrival we were greeted by the doorman who just happened to be Joe Louis (the Brown Bomber) former Heavy Weight Boxing Champion of the World.

As we had a bit of time to kill before we could check into the rooms we went for a stroll around the casino where we watched Telly Savalas (Kojak) who's pile of chips got bigger with every game he played.

When we checked into the rooms I was absolutely gobsmacked, I had never seen anything like it and thought to myself " Let the party begin "

We went to see Tom Jones who was performing at the hotel. Unfortunately, he declined our invitation to party with us so we carried on without him.

On our arrival back to Seattle we all went for a meal at the Black Angus (again courtesy of Big Mike) He then decided we should carry on the party downtown so after a visit to the back of his car, where he pulled out a shoe box full of money and gave us a wad each. I counted my wad it was $300. That evening I spent $150 and I remember the next day saying to a Manny Matos that I still had money left. He said he did too so we went downtown and did a bit of shopping.

The 77 season started much like the previous 3 seasons with a 1-0 loss away to Hawaii (at least we had an extra day there to get over it)

I started off the season at RB and we lost our first 3 games winning only 2 out of the first 8. The turning point came when Jimmy brought Mel Machin in at RB and moved me into the middle of the park to add a bit more steel for an away game in Dallas. My job was to screen the back four, win it and give it to the more creative players like Buttle and Jenkins. We won the game 1-0 and went on to win 6 out of the next 7 games.

In July the New York Cosmos came into town and Pele had now been joined by another World Cup winner Franz Beckenbauer and in front of 41,270 we won the game 1-0 with a goal from Jocky Scott and a clean sheet from Tony Chursky. At the end of the game, Pele gave me his shirt.

We won 5 out of the last 7 regular season games as Jimmy added the final piece of the jigsaw when he brought in Tommy Ord from our rivals the Vancouver Whitecaps and he scored 5 goals in the last 6 games to see us into the playoffs.

As well as moving me into midfield Jimmy also made me team captain and I would like to quote my good friend Tony Chursky from his contribution to my book Eternal Blue Forever Green.

The 1977 season began with major transitions. Our former coach, John Best, answered the call to become the new general manager of the Vancouver Whitecaps and Jimmy Gabriel, our team captain, and lion-like leader, became the new head coach. Jimmy saw in Adrian qualities, not unlike those in himself – a fiery, competitive spirit, a dedicated, loyal servant to the club, a positive, supportive voice and a ruthless, intimidating tackler. Not surprisingly, Jimmy named Adrian as our new captain, and our most successful season yet got underway.

THE PLAYOFFS

As in 76 our playoff campaign started in Vancouver, we had finished the season strong and went into the game quietly confident that we could do the business. Our last two games of the season we beat Hawaii 5-0 in front of 26,833 in the Kingdome and I opened the scoring with my second goal of the season (a 100% improvement over my previous season goals tally) and the other goals came from Buttle, Butler, Cave and Robertson. We then went to LA and won 4-2 with goals from Butler, Cave and Ord 2.

Going up against Vancouver was a big game for me, I had family and friends there and I still knew most of their players. I was really surprised when Jimmy was able to pick Tommy Ord up from Vancouver late in the season, he had always caused us a few headaches and with him in our team I thought we would have to much in the bag for them. The big threat from them I thought would come from little Derek Posse the ex Millwall great who had finished the season in double figures. However on the night we blocked him out and went onto win quite comfortable 2-0 with goals from Machin and yes that man Tommy Ord!

The other thing I remember about the game was that we had to pull the brawling Mike England and Jimmy Robertson apart in the dressing room after the game. I looked at it as no bad thing because it said to me although we won the game we could still do better.

It was now onto Minnesota who beat us in both regular season games. We knew going into the game it would be a tough place to get a result but felt if we could win there we always fancied our chances back in the Kingdome in front of our incredible fans. Goals from Butler and Ord in front of 35,899 and a tremendous team effort saw us come out on top 2-1, so it was back to Seattle for the second leg. This was another tight game and in front of 42,091 Sounders fans we won 1-0 on a goal from Tommy Ord, his fourth consecutive goal.

After good results against Vancouver and Minnesota, we were now through to the semi-final, two games away from being in the Soccer Bowl Final in Portland.

Four days later we played the LA Aztecs at the Rose Bowl in front of a measly 9,115 fans.

LA were the pundits favourites and everyone was hoping for a Aztecs Vs Cosmos final which would have seen the Great George Beat up against the Legendary Pele.

The Aztecs had a star-studded cast lead by superstar George Best who had come to the States to resurrect his career. They were a very experienced side that boasted players that were big names in the UK, Ron Davies, Phil Beal, Terry Mancini and the wizardry of Charlie Cooke plus the leading goal scorer Steve David.

I think this was probably my best game as a Sounders player. Head Coach Jimmy Gabriel gave me the task of man-marking Bestie and I think we surprised a lot of people by winning 3-1 with goals from Buttle, Cave and Robertson and I was voted Man of the Match.

We had our usual celebration after the game but knew it would still be a difficult home tie.

I remember getting up the next morning and going to breakfast, as I did I picked up a newspaper to take a look at the match report but instead ended up reading an article on Elvis who had passed away a few days earlier and I felt quite sad as I had always been a big fan of his. As I headed back to my room, I couldn't believe my eyes when I bumped into someone I knew from my hometown of Colchester, Ken Goody, who had been at the game the previous night. He told me he would be sure to let everyone back home know that I was voted Man of the Match. We then proceeded to have our photo taken with Jimmy Robertson and Micky Cave alongside Evil Knievel's car that was parked outside the hotel that we were staying in. Unfortunately we didn't get to see him, I guess he must have been catching up on his beauty sleep.

It was then back to Seattle where in 4 days time we would play the second leg to see who would go through to the final in Portland.

There was a great buzz around the City but Jimmy used his experience to make sure we were well rested and everything we did was about making sure we didn't pickup any silly injuries and that we all understood our individual and collective roles.

As team captain, I had to leave training early the day before the game along with Jimmy and Jack Daley to attend a press luncheon that was also attended by our LA counter parts that included George Best. It was quite nice because I actually got the chance to talk to George on a one to one basis.

At the luncheon I was asked by one of the reporters if I had any special plans to stop George again and I think I just replied by saying that I hoped I could just stay this close to him as I followed him into the toilet.

It was game time the atmosphere in the stadium was

electric, the lads were going around to one another in the dressing room saying those last words I had heard so many times before only this time they seemed to just echo ALL THE BEST. These 3 words were later to become the title of a book about the Sounders written by Doug Thiel.

As I lead the team out the noise level went up another notch and as usual the hair on the back of my neck stood to attention during the National Anthem. My nerves soon settled down as the game kicked off and I just kept saying to myself " Concentration " We won the game 1-0 with a goal from Jocky Scott and at the end of the game, the crowd of 56,256 just erupted into cheers that almost lifted the roof off the stadium. It was really emotional as we did our lap of honour, I will never forget the big smiles on the faces of my teammates Tommy Ord and Jocky Scott and wishing if only we could take this crowd to Portland with us.

I think winning 4-1 on aggregate sent a message that we were up for the challenge of the Cosmos and that although we respected them, we did not fear them. We knew going into the LA game that the Cosmos would be our opponents as they had played the night before and in front of 73,000 they beat Rochester 4-1 winning 6-2 on aggregate. I think knowing that it was New York in the final and that it would be Pele's last game in the NASL only added to the intensity of our game with LA as every player gave his all on the night.

After the poor start to the season, we were all delighted for Jimmy, Bobby and Harry who had kept the faith and belief that on our day we could compete with the best.

The following day we traveled to Portland and that evening we just had a meal and a quiet night in the hotel. The day before the game we went to the ground for a light session and caught the back end of the Cosmos session. In the evening both teams attended a banquet. The Commissioner Phil Woosnam, along with other NASL dignitaries and the World Media were there and it became a bit of an Evening with the NewYork Cosmos as the talk was all about it being Pele's last NASL game followed by Franz Beckenbauer being presented with the league's MVP award. I remember thinking to myself are we in this F***ing Final or what? After the meal and other bullshit, it was back to the hotel to get rested up for the big day.

TWO KEY PLAYERS

Tony Chursky – The Poetry Man Tony joined the Sounders in 76. We became really good friends when we first played together for the Vancouver Spartans in 1972. At this time he was also attending Simon Fraser University where he was starting to develop a reputation as a very good up and coming young keeper.

After I got suspended for six weeks my Spartans roommates and I moved in with Tony and his family in North Delta. You can read more about our time together in my book Eternal Blue Forever Green.

I knew through playing with Tony for the Spartans that he had tremendous potential and my thoughts were confirmed when he was selected to a BC select team to play against Santos of Brazil and World Cup winner Pele! I was really disappointed myself not to be able to play as it was during my six weeks suspension. On the night Tony had an excellent game and I knew then he would go onto bigger and better things.

Just before Tony finished his degree I spoke with John Best about him only to find out that John already had him pencilled in as a replacement for Barry Watling.

Tony had a really good first season for the Sounders and was instrumental in us getting to the Soccer Bowl Final.

Steve Buttle – The Wizard Steve and I were both East

Anglia boys through and through, Steve from Norwich and me from Colchester. We first met when he played for Ipswich Town youth team and I for Colchester United youth team. To look at him, you might not have him down as a soccer player, but boy how wrong you would have been! Steve could truly play and had a magical wand for a left foot. Being a lefty I think he gave us a nice balance in midfield whether he played out wide or more tucked in where we could get him on the ball more.

Before joining the Sounders for the 77 season he played at Bournemouth where the Sounders coaching staff Gabriel, Howe and Redknapp knew all about him.

Much more about Steve in Eternal Blue Forever Green.

SOCCER BOWL 77

In reaching the final, we had put together a run of seven wins, it now came down to this final game. When we were in the dressing room getting ready to go out I couldn't help but think back to the day I sat on the bench for Hillingdon in the 1971 FA Trophy Final at Wembley. Although I was only 19 years old then, I thought I might never get the chance again to play in such a prestigious game and the disappointment left some deep scars.

It now seemed such a distant memory, as I stood in the tunnel with my heart pounding and and my stomach tied in knots. The chanting of the fans could be heard rocking the seats all around us. All the other familiar sights and sounds faded. I was game ready. Focused. I had to be. My career was summed up in this moment. This was the Championship play-off game and I would come up against three World Cup Winners Pele, Carlos Alberto and Beckenbauer. Pele! The soccer player that still to this day is said to possibly be the best player of all time. Yes me, the boy from little old Colchester.

The cheers rose to a roar and flags waved in the stands. Since the game was only a couple of hours drive for our supporters, there seemed to be more local fans than for New York. As the lads and I strode onto the pitch, I remember thinking this is for you, Our Fans! Who had started on the journey back in 74. It was my proudest soccer moment, shared with the best team I had played on and with such a great bunch of lads.

Unlike in the two Aztecs games, Jimmy didn't really delegate the job of man-marking Pele as he had wanted me to do on George Best, he simply said " You know he will come into your area so just try to stop him from turning, stay on your feet and don't dive in " I remember my biggest fear was that I might make a mistake that would cost us, but fortunately, although we lost the game I didn't make that dreaded error.

I thought we started the game really well and in the first 20 minutes created 2 or 3 good chances. In fact, we had the ball in the back of the net when Shep Messing could only push a tremendous shot from Jocky Scott onto the crossbar and Micky Cave was there to head it in, but to our despair, the referee disallowed it for offside. The Cosmos took the lead when Tony Chursky gave the ball up cheaply – I remember at the time feeling sorry for Tony, but in true Chursky style he put it behind him and went onto have a super game. At about the half hour mark I won a tackle around the 35 yard line that lead to us equalizing. After some really good combination play that involved Cave, Scott and Ord the latter calmly slotted it past Messing. I remember the half time being very positive and we felt we were a bit unfortunate not to be in front.

Fifteen minutes into the second half Pele had a good chance, but fortunately for us he put it over the crossbar. We continued to push forward and we're still creating chances. With about 15 minutes left, Jimmy brought on super sub Dave Butler for Micky Cave. The Cosmos took the lead with about 12 minutes remaining when Chinaglia headed in from Man of the Match Steve Hunts cross. Shortly after I felt I let myself down when I kicked out at Tony Field when he was on the ground with the ball between his legs. It was a bit of pay back for him going over the top on me during the regular season game in the Kingdome and then Pele had to get between Chinaglia and me when Chinaglia started giving it large over the incident.

Jimmy also brought on Tommy Jenkins to try and get us back into the game and with five minutes left we hit them on the counter-attack only for Jocky to go inches wide with his effort. I think had Dave Gillett's 30 yard scorcher and the one Steve Buttle hit the post with had gone for us, I think it might have been a different outcome.

At the final whistle, all I remember was fans running onto the field towards Pele and him being lifted into the air. I just felt the exact opposite to how I had felt a few days earlier when we beat LA in the Kingdome. I was gutted, I felt drained and especially disappointed for our fans, but in that same moment I felt so proud of my teammates who had given their all on the day!

After a bit of reflection in the dressing room, we returned to the hotel where as captain I accepted our Trophy as the Pacific Northwest Champions. We flew out of Portland at about 10:30 pm and the reception we got back at Sea Tac Airport was just incredible. It was all then back to Jimmy Gabriel's house where we partied through the night.

MEMORIES BY WERNER ROTH

TEAM CAPTAIN NY COSMOS

1972 – 79

What I remember most about the 77 Final is how nervous I was due to the fact that it was Pele's last match and we were so invested in winning him a Championship.

I hated the stadium, the poor synthetic turf and that we were playing the Sounders.

As we were walking out of the tunnel I was trying to shake the nervousness off when Pedro Garra our chief of security, who was leading the officials and both teams out into the stadium, tripped over a television cable and went head over heels, we all started laughing and it immediately broke all the tension. I think this is why right from the start it was such a great game.

THE TEAM

The Captain

Adrian Webster, the Sounders captain, is now playing a new role as a defensive midfielder. Head coach Jim Gabriel moved Adrian into his new role for the road game in Dallas June 2 and the Sounders have lost only one game since to climb back into the Western Division race.

As a young lad, I had always dreamed of playing professional football for Tottenham Hotspur's and for my country. It didn't quite work out that way, but my journey took me to North America where I played for the Seattle Sounders playing with and against some of the greats of the game. This was the best team I had played on, they were a great bunch of lads who bonded on and off the field and were proud to wear the Blue and Green of the Sounders. I would like to share a few memories about each one.

1 GK TONY CHURSKY – The Poetry Man

Tony is one of the nicest and most sincere people I have ever met and a very good friend. I first met him when we played together for the Vancouver Spartans in the BC Premier League.

In 1976 Tony replaced the very popular Barry Watling. I feared Tony might find it tough taking over from the very experienced Watling but it was not long before the fans were asking " Barry who? " He wasn't the biggest keeper but he was very brave, had great agility and was a very good shot stopper. I think what gave him the edge over Barry who was a very good line keeper was that Tony had tremendous spring and wasn't intimidated when going for crosses in the box.

Tony went on to have a very good career in both the NASL and the MISL and in 2005 he was inducted into the Canadian Hall of Fame. He is now retired and still lives in the area with his wife Donna and we have remained good friends over the years.

4 RB MEL MACHIN – Mr. Class

Mel came to the Sounders on loan from Norwich City and slotted into the back four considered to be one of the best in the league. In his only season he played a key role in getting us to the final. As a defender, he read the game well and was very good at intercepting the ball and breaking forward with it. He was very comfortable with the ball and his decision making was first class. A really nice guy who oozed class on and off the field.

At the end of the season, he returned to England where he had a very successful Managerial career. In 2002 he was voted into the Norwich City Hall of Fame.

17 CB DAVE GILLETT – Chopper

In my opinion Dave was the most consistent player through the first 4 seasons. He and I were the only two players that played in the final that also played in the Sounders very first league game in 74.

A Scotsman from Edinburgh he was a six – foot plus no – nonsense defender who was good in the air, fierce in the tackle, had a good range of passing and as he showed in the final he could play a bit. Under the guidance of fellow Scot Jimmy Gabriel and playing alongside the former Spurs legend Mike England he took his game to another level.

He is now retired and plays a lot of golf with Jimmy Gabriel and is another one I have remained good friends with over the years.

5 CB MIKE ENGLAND – Big Mike

Mike joined the Sounders in 1975 from Tottenham Hotspur. Considered to be one of the all time greats in England where he played 300 games for the mighty Spurs and 44 games for Wales. Playing alongside Dave Gillett they formed one of the best partnerships in the NASL and it was a privilege to play two seasons in a back four of Webster, Gillett, England and Stephens. He was dominant in the air stopped his opponent from turning, won tackles and used the ball well, in fact he made all the difficult things look easy. He was voted by his peers into the NASL All-Star First Team 4 consecutive seasons. In 1986 he received an MBE for his contribution to Welsh Football and in 2013 he was inducted into the Tottenham Hall of Fame.

3 LB JIMMY McALISTER – Jimmy Mac

Although most teams in the NASL were made up of experienced foreign players, Jimmy was the first local boy to break into the Sounders starting lineup. He got his first taste of first team soccer when he made 2 appearances in the 76 season. In 77 he was an integral part of the team's success in reaching the Soccer Bowl Final. In the final, he was up against the very experienced Tony Field and he never gave him a look in and so impressed was Pele that he gave him his shirt. 77 was a great season for Jimmy who was awarded Rookie of the Year as well as making his debut for the US National team.

19 RW JIMMY ROBERTSON – Robbo

One of my favourite players to play for the Sounders. An exciting tricky winger who on his day was unplayable, he was brave had pace and was a good crosser of the ball. He was a Scottish International who made his name playing for Tottenham and Arsenal being the first player to score for both teams. In his first season with the Sounders, he broke his leg from a brutal tackle playing against the Philadelphia Atoms. He returned the following season and played a big part in taking us to the Final.

The last I heard of Robbo was that he was working for a Computer Insurance Company in Staffordshire.

2 M/F JOCKY SCOTT – The Black Pirate

Another Scotsman who before coming to Seattle made over 300 appearances for Dundee and Aberdeen scoring 130 goals. He was later inducted into the Dundee FC Hall of Fame.

His attitude and application was superb and he always worked tirelessly for the team. When Jimmy signed Tommy Ord, Jocky played in the number 10 role getting forward to link up with Cave and Ord and slotting back in alongside Buttle and myself to do the dirty work. In 39 games for the Sounders, he scored 9 goals and had 11 assists. He was a great character and fun to be around, I think he inherited the nickname Black Pirate for his rugged looks. After his playing career, he had an extensive management career as well as coaching in both Scotland and England. I met up with Jocky when he was the Manager of Notts County when they came to Colchester for a league game. We enjoyed a couple of beers after the game and reminisced about our playing days for the Sounders.

15 M STEVE BUTTLE – The Wizard

Steve soon became a favourite of the fans both on and off the field. Physically there was nothing of him, but he could turn a six foot – two giant into a four foot – two dwarf with his performances. He was so comfortable on the ball and very seldom gave it away. In fact, he seldom gave it to me! He used to say you win it and give it to me!

After a spell of playing for the Pittsburgh Spirit in the MISL he returned to the Sounders where he made another Soccer Bowl appearance in 82 again losing to the New York Cosmos.

I was saddened to hear that in June 2012 Steve passed away after a long battle with cancer aged 59. A memorial service was held in Seattle celebrating his life. I feel very privileged to have played with Steve and to have shared so many good times.

RIP LEGEND!

18 F TOMMY ORD – Ordy

Tommy moved to the NASL in 1972 when he joined the Montreal Olympique from Chelsea. I remember playing against him on a couple of occasions and John Best saying in his pre- match briefing how we needed to be aware of him at set pieces.

At 5' 10" he was not the biggest of forwards, but was very good in the air. He had the knack of getting up early and of being able to ' hang ' and still get in a powerful header on goal. His touch and hold – up play was also very good plus he scored goals.

When he joined us we were heading towards the playoffs and he was the final piece of the jigsaw puzzle!

He scored 9 goals in 12 games including the goal in the 2-1 loss in the final.

Tommy joined the Buffalo Stallions in the MISL and in 1982 I signed him for the Phoenix Inferno when I took over as Head Coach.

12 F MICKY CAVE – Cavey

Micky joined the Sounders from Bournemouth. In 76 he helped the Los Angeles Skyhawks win the ASL title. He wasn't your typical big English battling ramp CF but more of a thinking player who played off the shoulder of defenders and caused them problems with his movement.

In his first season, he scored 12 regular season goals and 1 in the playoffs. He and Tommy Ord formed a good partnership and they lead the line for us in reaching the final. He played 75 games scoring 31 goals before moving onto the Pittsburgh Spirit in the MISL.

I was still in Phoenix the night I got the call from Steve Buttle to say that Micky had passed away and that he had discovered his body when he failed to show for training. It was the 6th November 1984 it was my 33rd birthday and I remember Steve and I shed a few tears as we tried to deal with this tragic loss. Micky was a bubbly person who enjoyed life and like Steve was starting to carve out a career in coaching. However, I know he will always be remembered in Seattle, for the contribution he made in helping us reach the Soccer Bowl Final in Portland.

As a tribute, the Player of the Year Award was later named after him at Bournemouth.

RIP Cavey!

SUBS

6 M TOMMY JENKINS – Jenks

Tommy joined the Sounders for the 76 season, he was a former teammate of Jimmy Gabriel at Southampton. He was slim in stature, had really quick feet, could pick a pass and was a defenders nightmare when he ran at you with the ball. It was great watching him drag the ball from one foot to another and with a change of pace be gone or hit a pinpoint pass.

Unfortunately, although we saw glimpses of that magic, I don't think Seattle really saw the best of him due to a chronic injury and even after surgery he never really got that sharpness back. Tommy was another one who did countless hours of PR work, which I think was to help him later when he finished playing and got into coaching. Tommy and Dave Gillett worked together for the Seattle Storm and when the league folded Tommy continued to coach in Washington State before being recruited by Jimmy Mac to coach for Seattle United.

8 F DAVE BUTLER – Musky

Dave joined us five games into the inaugural season and soon became a favourite with the fans. He was the perfect player to play off of Big John with his energetic linkup play and dynamic runs into the box and in his first season he scored 9 goals.

Dave was very bubbly and loved to tell a joke, but on the other side of the coin, he was a worry wart which I think later on cost him his starting role. He went onto play 97 games scoring 34 goals for the Sounders and he played his part coming off the bench during the playoffs and the final.

Dave continued his playing days in the MISL playing for Pittsburgh, Baltimore, Kansas and Philadelphia. He returned to the Sounders in 1983 to coach the reserve team where he also played one more first team game.

The last time I saw Dave was at the reunion game in the Kingdome against the Vancouver Whitecaps in front of 33,000 organized by John Best.

11 RW PAUL CROSSLEY – Road Runner

Paul joined the Sounders for the start of the 75 season after making over 200 appearances for Tranmere Rovers in England. He quickly became a favourite with the fans with his pacy runs past the opposing fullbacks.

With the arrival of Jimmy Robertson and a change in the system, Paul found himself making fewer appearances as the whole league was starting to bring the big names over. He made 77 appearances scoring 16 goals before he moved onto the Baltimore Blast in the MISL. He finished his playing career with the Blast making 105 appearances scoring 45 goals. After his playing career he was assistant coach at Loyola College and in 1991 he became Head Coach of Shoreline Community College.

Paul passed away in 1996 aged 47. At the time of his death by heart attack, he had compiled a 46 – 30 – 17 record.

RIP Paul. Thanks for the memories!

14 D MANNY MATOS – Manno

Manny was the Sounders first pick in the 1975 NASL College Draft. He attended Adelphi University where he played on the schools 1974 NCAA Men's Division II Championship team. He was a no – nonsense defender and what he lacked in finesse he more than made up for with a tremendous determination to do well.

The 77 season turned out to be a very frustrating season for him. After working so hard to establish himself as a starter he had to have surgery on his groin which kept him out for the season.

During our Soccer Bowl campaign, Manny worked with radio and television sportscaster Wayne Cody commentating on our games. He was also instrumental in the Sounders off-season program where he became a household name.

He played one more season for the Sounders before

moving onto the Los Angeles Skyhawks and finally the Buffalo Stallions in the MISL where he eventually retired from the game.

Although Steve Hunt was voted Man of the Match for his goal and assist, on the day I thought Shep Messing was Superb and he has kindly shared his thoughts.

SHEP MESSING GK for the COSMOS

In 1971, it became known as " The Fight ", matching unbeaten heavyweights Joe Frazier and Muhammad Ali at Madison Square Garden. It takes two great opponents in any sport competing in a championship to bring out the best in both and to make for a contest that's always remembered. When my friend Adrian Webster asked me to comment on our game from 40 years ago, that's how I view the 1977 NASL Soccer Bowl between the Cosmos and the Sounders.

The Cosmos in 1977 were the toast of New York, of the country and perhaps of the world. The very same Muhammad Ali, along with Mick Jagger, Robert Redford and Elton John now followed our team as fans.

The Cosmos were the first team of " galacticos " including 3 World Cup Winners, Pele, Franz Beckenbauer and Carlos Alberto. Two of them, Franz and Carlos had been captains of their World Cup winning teams and of course Pele, who had been on his World Cup winning Brazilian team an unprecedented 3 times.

The Seattle Sounders were the opposite of us in terms of style, flair and composition. They were an all-star combination of English, Scottish, American and Canadian talent with a heart and a work rate better than ours. With Tony Chursky in goal, Wales international Mike England an imposing figure in central defence and Adrian Webster as their captain orchestrating the midfield, they were always going to be difficult to break down. Jocky Scott, Tommy Ord, Steve Buttle and Micky Cave were a nightmare to defend against.

We had played them earlier that season at the Kingdome in Seattle in front of over 41,000 raucous fans. We lost 1-0 on a Jocky Scott header but it easily could have been 3-0. Everyone in our locker room knew that this was going to be a battle to the end. So how did I feel, a kid from the streets of the Bronx, New York, about to go onto a championship game with three legends as my teammates?

I went to speak to each one of them privately in our Portland hotel the night before the game. Maybe just to calm my nerves, or get some advice or maybe hoping to have some of their greatness rub off on me.

Pele was first and he smiled as he always did, a smile

that could light up a room as we sat on the balcony. He was himself an unbelievable goalkeeper with athleticism that was unworldly. He always says he was a better goalkeeper than me and I'm sure that he's right. His advice to me was simple. " Shepito – don't worry about the shots on target – but the shots that are going wide of the goal – don't pull them into the goal. "

Then he laughed forever – he thought that was pretty funny

I went to see Carlos Alberto in the corner of the hotel bar (he called it his office) He was always cool, calm and elegant with a smile on his face as well. Any advice for tomorrow, Carlos?

" Let me tell you what's going to happen, Sheppy. On the first corner kick for Seattle, Mike England and the rest of them are going to come flying in hard at you. Go hard, go get the ball and then hold it. There will be ten players all inside the 6 yard box around you. But don't kick it out to clear it. Put the ball down at my feet in the 6 yard box with everyone around me and I'll take care of the rest. "

I couldn't tell if he was joking or not…but knowing Carlos, I'm pretty sure that he wasn't.

I saved the Kaiser, Franz, for last. He was in his room with a healthy snack and preparing for tomorrow. His advice was serious and to the point. He sat me down and said " Shep, every player goes into a big game with three things on his mind. 1. Don't let me make a mistake that costs us the game. 2. Let me just do my job, nothing bad, nothing special, just do my job. 3. Let me be the one that makes the play, seizes the moment and wins the game. I never think about 1 and 2. I always think about number 3.

You tomorrow, think about number 1 and don't screw up. "

Thanks a lot Franz!

Now we're ready to go and play in what turned out to be the greatest game of our lives. Adrian Webster was and still is a man of huge talent, commitment, leadership and character. He was the captain of a great Seattle Sounders team that captured the imagination and laid the foundation for the city, the team and the entire northwest that remains today. I'm honoured to be able to share these thoughts and contribute to Adrian's cause. You will always be the captain my friend.

Thanks for the contribution and kind words Shep. You are a class act!

PELE'S FAREWELL GAME

Our 77 season actually finished in late September when we had the privilege to play against Santos Pele's only other club in a warm up game in the Kingdome in front of 21,179 before they went onto play the Cosmos at Giants Stadium in Peles Farewell game. After missing out on playing against Santos a few years earlier in Vancouver, it was another boyhood dream come true for me.

The game at Giants Stadium was attended by Muhammad Ali, Bobby Moore and a host of other celebrities. It was televised on ABC's Wide World of Sports and I watched it with my Sounders teammates. As part of the buildup they showed how Pele had become the number one player in the World, as well as him being interviewed on a talk show and showing his juggling skills with a grapefruit. He played the first half for the Cosmos and the second half for Santos. The Cosmos won the game 2-1 with Pele scoring from a free-kick.

MY IDOLS

Playing in the NASL gave me the opportunity to play against my two idols!

This book would certainly not be complete in my eyes if I didn't talk about what was truly my greatest footballing pleasure and privilege – the chance to play against the King of Soccer **PELE!**

As an 11 year old schoolboy growing up in Colchester in the early 60's I remember writing a piece on the Brazilian National Team and the young Pele, for a social studies project. Little did I know then, that I would actually end up playing against the great man – not once, but four times.

Pele was 17, when he won his first World Cup in Sweden in 1958. During his career, he scored 1,281 goals in 1,363 games and won 3 World Cups. He played all his career for Santos before joining the New York Cosmos in 1975. He made 638 appearances for Santos, scoring an incredible 619 goals and in 92 games for Brazil, he scored 77 goals.

I honestly thought I had missed my chance to play against him when Santos came to Vancouver to play shortly after my arrival in Vancouver, as I was suspended. After the game, we went back to the hotel where Santos were staying and I was able to get his autograph. I remember thinking to myself this is probably the closest I will ever get to him and being surprised that at 5' 9", I was actually taller than him. I had always thought of him as being a giant!

The first time I did actually take to the field against him, was in his first season playing in the NASL for the New York Cosmos. The game was nationally televised and we won 2-0. The second game, was the opening of the Kingdome in front of 58,000 with Jimmy Gabriel scoring the first goal to be scored there and Pele putting on a clinic. The third occasion, was our regular season game again in the Kingdome in front of 41,000. We won 1-0 and after the game, Pele gave me his shirt. The fourth game, was the 77 Soccer Bowl Final at the Civic Stadium in Portland. The crowd was 35,000 and we lost 2-1'in what was Pele's last game in the NASL.

As I said earlier, playing in the NASL gave me the opportunity to play with and against some of the greats in the game. Next to Pele my other all-time favourite player was **GEORGE BEST.**

The first time I got to see him play live, was as a schoolboy, when my dad took me along to watch Ipswich Town Vs Manchester United. My other recollection was the night I watched Manchester United win the European Cup by beating Benfica 4-1 in May 1968. I watched the game on TV around our house with my best mates and of course, my dad! I remember it being a tight game and it going into extra time. Three minutes into extra time, George picked the ball up about 25 yards from the goal before carrying it into the penalty area where he dribbled around the keeper and rolled it into the empty net.

George came over to the US in 1976 to try to resurrect a career that was being dragged down by his boozing and womanizing. I remember being really excited about having the chance to play against my other idol. Not long after he arrived, we were scheduled to play the LA Aztecs in a couple of pre-season exhibition games and I remember George putting me on my arse a couple of times. George worked really hard to get himself in shape and for the first time in a couple of seasons, I think he fell back in love with the game. My biggest thrill playing against George, was in the first leg of the Soccer Bowl semifinal in the Rose Bowl, we won 3-1 and I was voted Man of the Match for my man marking job on him.

As a player George had it all. He had the ability to go

by players both ways (in the days when tackling above the waist was not always a card-able offence) two great feet, a change of pace, very good in the air, brave, and he could pull a bird. I think if he was playing today, he would probably be the first £100,000,000 player!

During the 70's we saw some of the all-time greats come over to play in the NASL and I have made a list of who I think were the best 10 I had the privilege to play against:

1. **PELE 2. GEORGE BEST 3. JOHAN CRUYFF 4. FRANZ BECKENBAUER 5. EUSEBIO**
6. **BOBBY MOORE 7. GERD MULLER 8. VLADISLAV BOGICEVIC 9. CARLOS ALBERTO**

    10. JOHAN NEESKENS

1978 SEASON

After a tremendous run at the end of the 77 season, where we W11 L3 to go to the Soccer Bowl Final, there was a real buzz about the place and expectations were high for the 78 season.

Not returning were D. Mel Machin and M. Jimmy Robertson, two very experienced players who had been key players in last seasons success.

Returning was M/F Jocky Scott and a key player from the 76 squad M/F Gordon Wallace and joining the team was new boy D. Les Parodi.

Our opening game of the season, was at home to the

Colorado Caribous, the crowd was 29,105 and although we won 3-0 it was a big blow when Dave Gillett was carried off with a broken leg.

It turned out to be a horrible season for both Dave and I, as 13 games into the season, I needed to have surgery on a very painful arthritic big toe that would keep me out for 9 months.

I was now playing the best soccer of my career and Dave as I have already said had been in my opinion the most consistent player over the first four seasons. It was a frustrating time for the both of us and we spent the rest of the season watching the games from the stands and enjoying those glorious sunny summer afternoons out by the pool.

The team struggled to make the playoffs, however qualified with a W15 L15 record. They traveled to New York where they lost 5-2 to the Cosmos in front of 47,780 in Giants Stadium.

The highlight of a very disappointing season was the arrival of England World Cup Captain Bobby Moore with 7 games left. From a purely soccer perspective it was a pleasure watching two of the games finest CB's, Bobby Moore and Mike England playing together. Both were 37 years old but played with the enthusiasm of two 17 year olds and there class was crystal clear for all to see as they passed the ball for fun on the Astro Turf in the Kingdome

1979 SEASON

BR: Walter Daggatt(man. Gen. Partner), John Anderson(trainer), Frank Barton, Derek
Smethurst, Bruce Rudroff, John Impey, Cliff Brown, Mike Ivanow, Mike England,
Al Trost, Ian Bridge, Ron Davies, Jack Daley(gen man), Keith Askenasi(PR)
FR: Jim McAlister, Bruce Miller, Steve Buttle, Paul Crossley, Alan Hudson, Harry
Redknapp(ass.coach), Jim Gabriel(coach), Bobby Howe(ass.coach), Adrian Webster,
Mickey Cave, Tommy Ord, John Ryan, Jimmy Neighbour

The 79 season was to be my last season with the club
and it proved to be a real roller coaster ride. It started
with the players strike, but before that I had worked
really hard in pre-season to get back into the team after
having surgery midway through the 78 season. During
the off season I had several discussions with Jimmy
Gabriel about a coaching position should I not be able
to continue playing. Although I thought the offer was a
really good safety net should that be the case I was
really pleased the pre-season went well and I was back
in the team.

After a disastrous 78 season Jimmy knew he had to

bring someone in to lift the morale of the team and the fans so when he secured the signature of Alan Hudson, optimism for the 79 season was high.

I was really excited about having the chance to play alongside this massive talent, in addition to my other midfield partner Steve Buttle. Unfortunately, we lost our first two games of the season and things turned even more sour when we got the call to go on strike. In the lead up to the strike GK Tony Chursky our player rep was shipped out to the California Surf. I replaced Tony only to find myself out of the team for the following 13 games, being told by the coaching staff that they felt after my surgery I had lost a yard or two of pace. Unbelievable!

The strike itself only lasted a few days but because of the divide in the camp the team never really got back on track, we failed to make the playoffs and attendances dropped below 18,000.

THE STRIKE

When it came to selecting our player rep all the players felt that Tony Chursky was the right person to represent us. He had graduated from Simon Frazer University in British Columbia, he was well spoken, a cool head and he had convinced us why it was in our best interest to have a union and we trusted that he would put our points of view forward. Unfortunately for him, it came at a time when he was negotiating a new contract with the club and the next thing we knew was that he had been shipped out to the California Surf. Tony was the first casualty!

We quickly called a meeting and it was decided I would take over his role and Steve Buttle would assist me.

The driving force behind forming a union was John Kerr, the Washington Diplomats player rep and Ed Garvey who had been involved with the NFL Players Union. The two came out to Seattle to meet with the players and to reinforce the message that Tony had conveyed, as well as to bring us up to date with what was happening at the other clubs.

The strike itself was never really about players wanting more money, but more about putting in place a standard set of rules and regulations across the league. It was well known amongst the players that there were certain clubs you wouldn't want to end up at. In some cases, you could be traded without having a say in the matter, or you might get injured and be without medical cover, as well as not get paid. We were lucky at Seattle, that none of those things were an issue and that is why today, I am proud of my teammates for making a stand, because by doing so, they were the pioneers for taking care of the welfare for all future players. Although the strike only lasted a few days, our efforts had not been in vain, as a few weeks later, the owners were forced to formally recognize our efforts and demands.

Shorty after the visit of Kerr and Garvey to Seattle, I attended a meeting of all the player reps in Washington DC, with a clear mandate from our lads, that if it came to a strike, we were all in. At the meeting, we were told to go back and talk to our teammates and let them know they should be prepared for strike action. When I got back to Seattle, I was informed that some of the lads had got ' Squeaky Bums ' and were not keen to strike, so we decided we would talk to Alan Hudson to make sure we still had his support. We felt that his high profile would give us more credibility and send a firm message to the owners that we were united in our decision. Al was brilliant about it and said he was with us all the way, the only thing he said was that he wanted to let Jimmy Gabriel know his decision first.

When word came through the strike was going ahead nationwide, a handful of the Sounders players decided that they were not going to support us, which inevitably caused a bit of friction and us hard-liners didn't hold back in letting them know our feelings.

We thought the timing of the strike was good for us as our next game was away to Dallas, so it wouldn't impact too much on our fans, even though the many we had spoken with fully supported our stand. Our biggest concern, was how long it might last, as some of the players had families to support. However single guys like Dave Gillett, Tommy Jenkins, Manny Matos, Tommy Ord and myself, said we were happy to help out financially.

Steve suggested that we needed to get in front of the media to put our point of view across, so we drafted a press release that I read out to the media at the training ground in Renton. I had no sooner finished delivering the statement, when the ' Scabs ' showed up for training. At this point, one or two of us had to be restrained, but not before delivering a good verbal blasting!

On the night of the Sounders game in Dallas, Alan Hudson invited all the non-playing ' rebels ' and their families to his house where he said to everyone " We have made our decision, we need to stick together and whatever the outcome, see it through. " I think that night his standing went up another notch in everyone's eyes. Some of the lads watched the game on TV, but most of us just played a bit of pool and had a couple of beers.

The strike was soon over and we were back into training. I'm not sure what Jimmy's thinking was, I suspect he wanted to get any animosity out of the way early as he organized a practice match and while Alan Hudson strutted his stuff, showing everyone who the number one player was, there was only one thing on my mind and that was to kick the arses of the scabs who thought they were coming in to take our shirts. The only player Jimmy kept on, was big Ron Davies, the former Southampton and Wales international who had been a teammate and good friend of Jimmy at the Dell. The rest of the scabs were released, which I think was Jimmy's way of showing his loyalty to us as well as helping his friend.

As I said, GK Tony Chursky was a central figure in the strike action and had it not been for the strike, I am sure the popular Chursky would have gone onto play many more games for the Sounders.

I firmly believe the strike took its toll on the Sounders season as we didn't make the playoffs and perhaps for different reasons, I think it lead to Jimmy, Harry and my departure.

Things appeared to be taking a positive turn when I was brought back into the team for the road trip to Detroit and Rochester. Jimmy told me he had brought me back into do a man-marking job on the Detroit danger man, Trevor Francis, a pacy forward over from England. Although we lost the game, I remember coming off the field well satisfied I had put in a good performance doing the job Jimmy had asked of me. The only thing Francis did on the night was to convert the penalty kick given when our GK Mike Ivanow brought down one of their players in the box.

Having secured my place back in the team, five games later, we traveled to New York where the team put in one of the best Sounders performances I have played in, with a brilliant 2-1 win over the Cosmos at Giants Stadium, to break their unbeaten run of 30 plus games. On the night Hudson and Buttle were superb and late in the game I remember beating Neeskens in he air to head the ball clear under pressure in our six yard box.

However, it all turned sour again for me when after playing in 10 of 11 games, in which we only won four I was not involved in the final four games of the season. Looking at the big picture and having been at the club for six seasons, I thought that maybe it was time for a change for both the club and I. The reasons included a divide in the camp, a breakdown in communication between Jimmy and I, which really hurt and in my opinion the increasing input Harry was having on team selection. If as I was told by the coaching staff, they felt I had lost a yard or two of pace, why was I then brought back into the team to do a man-marking job on the talented and very pacy Trevor Francis?

At the end of the season I went to see GM Jack Daley, as I felt I couldn't really talk to Jimmy. He had put his faith in Harry, who I felt didn't really want me in the team, as he had played a big part in bringing the much traveled Frank Barton over from England and he did all he could to make sure Frank started.

Jack told me that there were going to be some changes and suggested I should go away, take a break and we could talk when I got back. I listened to what Jack had to say, but there was an offer on the table to go and play for the Pittsburgh Spirit in the MISL. Because I felt my season had been a bit hit and miss and what I really needed was to be playing regularly I told Jack I had decided to take the offer. Not long after that Jimmy and Harry were gone too! Ah well that's football...

I have always been one to analyse my own performance after games and based on the Detroit and New York games and not the team's performance or the results, I just felt that if I was playing regular I could get back to my best. So at 28 years old , I went to Pittsburgh Pennsylvania, where I played 28 of the 32 games for the Spirit, scoring 3 goals and 6 assists in a really enjoyable season.

However, now looking back, I can't help but feel leaving the Sounders was like losing my best mate. At the end of the day, it was my decision to go to Pittsburgh, but I absolutely loved my time in Seattle and will always feel privileged to have been a Sounders player and to have played in the NASL.

JACK DALEY

General Manager Jack Daley was the longest serving member of the Sounders family, he was there for eight seasons. Jack could be quite an intimidating figure. He must have been about 6' 4", well built, not with what I would call an athletic frame, but a very confident man. When he had finished talking, you felt you had no other choice but to sign the contract. He loved the Sounders and during my six seasons I got to see several different sides to his personality.

One of my first memories was the club suits he chose they were Green with a yellow polo neck sweater and alternative check trousers, we looked like the Irish golf team. Right out of the Jack Daley catalogue!

As I have mentioned during the off season we did lots of appearances and I did several with him, for me, this was where he was at his best. I remember one in particular at a Rotary Club, Jack got up to speak first and as usual, he finished with a bit of humour. The President of the club then stood up and to everyone's disbelief told the same story Jack had just told! I can remember looking over at Jack and how we never cracked up, I will never know. I was tempted to tell the same story when I got up but thought better of it and we had a good laugh about it on the way home.

My former teammate and god friend, Dave Gillett and I were there from the beginning and I think Dave would agree when you get into management or coaching, you tend to look at the people that have influenced you. Both Dave and I took that pathway when we finished playing, Dave became Manager of the Seattle Storm and I Head Coach of the Arizona Condors and I am sure Jack, John and Jimmy were our role models. Before the current MLS Sounders were awarded a new franchise, I used to think how great it would be if Gillett and Webster became the new Daley and Best.

When I left the Sounders at the end of the 79 season, it wasn't exactly the fairy tale ending I had hoped for. It had been a difficult season, we didn't make the playoffs, the strike had left a few scars and there had been a few fall-outs along the way. However I will never forget when I went to see Jack at the end of the season about moving on, he knew it was a difficult decision for me to make and he said just go away for a few weeks and think about it, there will be changes and it might be in your best interest. However, there was an offer to go and play for the Pittsburgh Spirit in the MISL which I took up. There were changes Alan Hinton replaced Jimmy Gabriel, but I will never forget Jack did leave the door open for me to stay.

Thanks for the Great Memories Jack!

From Eternal Blue Forever Green

" The first time that Walt Daggatt, John Best and I had a joint meeting regarding the newly awarded soccer franchise from the NASL to the city of Seattle, was at the league meeting in Miami in January 1974. We discussed how we wanted to organize the franchise from an operational standpoint, as well as from a team concept and player development program, for an Inaugural season just four months away.

" As Head Coach, John Best was to take the lead on scouting and identifying the players who would be best suited to represent the franchise and ownership group in a city where the Sonics and Husky football dominated the media attention of a sports-hungry Pacific Northwest. Realizing the current popularity of the British rock bands, management elected to field a squad of young developing players from the lower divisions in Great Britain as well as other European free agents.

" In came Dave Butler and a group of Beatle style haircut lads with their engaging accents, to form the basis of a team with American College graduates and a select number of walk-ons.

In the free agent group, the Sounders wound up finding a prize. Down from Vancouver, came Adrian Webster, who John Best offered a contract to after seeing him play in a Cup Final in BC.

Winning the RB spot, Adrian served the Sounders well as a player on and off the field and in the community as part of the soccer clinic group which specialized in teaching soccer skills to the young and old.

In 1997, the new Head Coach, Jimmy Gabriel moved Adrian into midfield and made him the team captain, leading the team out in the 77 Soccer Bowl.

" Adrian was a key contributor in the Sounders launch to a winning season in their inaugural year, as well as a continued asset in the drive to become a playoff contender in the following seasons. A fierce competitor on the field, Webster was one of the nicest players off the field. Nice guys do finish first! "

Jack Daley.

CHAPTER SIX
The Hudson Era
Great Banter, Great Camaraderie

Alan Hudson's arrival in Seattle was certainly a big deal in every sense of the phrase. The consensus was how well Jimmy had done to secure his signature.

I first met Al when I played against him many years earlier playing for Colchester United's youth team against Chelsea's youth team in the South Eastern Counties League. Of course, back then, I couldn't have dreamed that 10 years later, I would get the chance to play alongside this super talent thousands of miles from home. I remember on the coach trip back to Colchester, all the conversation was about what a good player the young Huddy was and not that we had just played Chelsea youth team.

Al had fallen out with the Arsenal management after they lost in the 1978 FA Cup Final to Ipswich and arrived in Seattle for a £100,000 fee before our 1979 season started.

The Sounders players first encounter with him was at Renton Stadium, after an evening game against a local team that Jimmy had organized. The game was twofold one to keep us ticking over and two to take a look at a couple of young local boys.

The thing I remember most about that meeting was how Al just strolled into the dressing room after the game and went around introducing himself to everyone. I somehow knew straight away he was going to fit in well with our already tight-knit family and the players were left with a great first impression.

As I mentioned earlier, one of my first jobs as the

player rep, was to try to persuade Al to come out on strike with us if it came to it. It must be remembered that here was a top-class player, still at the peak of his powers, aged 27, trying to get his career back on track, having just signed a lucrative contract, purchased a new house and moved his family across the Atlantic. Why on earth would he want to go on strike?

From our point of view, we knew his support would give us far more credibility and when it happened, 18 of the 24 man squad walked out, one of which was Al. Not only did he participate, he invited all of us over to his home and rallied us with calls to stick together and to see it through, whatever the outcome. Many years later, Al confided in me that protecting his own personal situation never crossed his mind when he went to tell Jimmy his decision and that he would have always supported his teammates come what may.

Another thing I admired about Al, was the tremendous inner strength he had. When he arrived in Seattle, I already knew that not only did he play for England, but along with the late Great Bobby Moore, he could also drink for England. Joining us meant he didn't have to change his social habits! However what I didn't know was the level of fitness he was able to sustain while living the so called good life. I can honestly say that Al took our celebrations – win or lose – to another level. I must add, it was much better when we won as he really did hate to lose. In Al's first season, we had several Friday night games, meaning after the game it was straight up to the bar in the lounge at the Kingdome to start refueling and to mingle with the fans. In earlier days, it would then be off to a nightclub, or onto one of the many parties that were always going on. However this all changed when after one game Al invited everyone back to his house and it then became a regular post-game routine.

I remember after one Friday night game we went straight back to Al's place where we started our refueling, some played pool while Al was the DJ playing all the great collection of music he had.

The camaraderie between the guys was fantastic and the humour was hilarious. It was an environment whereby we could just kick back and not worry about what other people's perception of us was.

This particular night or should I say morning we crashed at about 7:00 am and I ended up sleeping on the floor in one of the spare bedrooms, only to be woken by Al a few hours later to be told we were off to Long Acres Racetrack in Renton. After a quick shower and a clean set of clothes provided by Al (from a wardrobe I think David Beckham would have been proud of) we took off to meet up with Harry Redknapp and a few of the other lads. First port of call was the bar where we had a beer while Harry told us the game plan, which was to follow a couple of punters around to see who they were betting on and then to place our own bets.

After a great day at the track it was back to Al's for the second half. This carried on through to early Sunday evening, before heading off home to get rested up for training Monday morning.

The banter in the dressing room Monday morning

would be hilarious as all the weekend activities would be shared with those that hadn't been involved. However, as soon as we stepped outside, Al would take on his other role ' Super Athlete ' He would grab my arm as we started running and say to me " Right up the front " and that is where we stayed, while in the background you could hear the moans and groans coming from John Ryan and his buddies as we set the pace! Fortunately, like Al, I loved to train, and it didn't matter what we had done on the weekend, we were both of the same mindset to put it all back in on the track. Al's fitness was amazing and it would certainly stand him in good stead later in his life. Many years later when I spoke to him about his horrific car accident in 1997, he told me he was convinced and this is backed up by the top medical team he had – that all those hours of football training over the years definitely helped him to survive the serious injuries he suffered.

Unfortunately I only played 10 games with Al for the Sounders as I did not play for 13 games after the strike and was left out the last four games of the season. I do believe under different circumstances the midfield trio of Hudson, Webster and Buttle would have been a match for any of the other other midfield setups in the league at that time.

At the end of the 79 season Jimmy was released and Alan Hinton took over the reins. The purse strings opened up and Hinton went about bringing in the supporting cast for Hudson. Under Hinton's guidance and Hudson's on field leadership, they went on to set a new record of games won in a season and in 1982 they reached the Soccer Bowl Final.

CHAPTER SEVEN
MISL BOUND

When joining the Pittsburgh Spirit in the MISL at the end of the 79 NASL season I felt that my last campaign with the Sounders had been a bit hit and miss, so I was really looking forward to getting some games in under my belt.

Alex Pringle was the Head Coach and I remember playing against the Scotsman when he played for the Tampa Bay Rowdies and the Washington Diplomats in the NASL. Upon my arrival, he asked me to recommend some of my Seattle teammates, which I was happy to do. We had a really good season. I played in 28 of the 32 games and we made the playoffs, losing to the eventual winners, the New York Arrows.

The season didn't start well and Alex was replaced by Len Bilous and his assistant John Kowalski, who had previous indoor experience. What they did was to get us better organized and showed us how to utilize the boards better. The games were played in ice hockey and and basketball arenas where the Astro Turf was laid over the ice and boards. We played our games at the Civic Arena in downtown Pittsburgh, which had a capacity of 16,940.

Like the Sounders we had some great characters – none more so than the former Rangers player, Graham Fyffe and Alfie Conn, the ex Rangers, Celtic and Tottenham forward. Between them, Fyffe and Conn scored 52 goals. Alfie like myself just played the one season while Graham went on to play for the Cleveland Force and the St Louis Steamers.

Unfortunately, the owner of the Spirit made the decision to suspend the entire operation for the following season and as I didn't want to sit out a season, I became a free agent. I had two offers, one from the Cleveland Force, where the former Chelsea favourite Eddie McCreadie was the Coach and who Alan Hudson later joined. The other offer was from a new franchise named the Phoenix Inferno.

I opted for the Inferno for two reasons. Firstly, it was

the highest monthly salary I had earned playing in the NASL and the MISL ($3,500 a month plus a car and an apartment) and secondly, the beautiful weather. Again, I was asked by the Coach, Norm Sutherland, to recommend a couple of my old teammates, which I did and I was joined by Dave Gillett and Tommy Jenkins. Norm had recruited Vic Davidson (ex Celtic), Willie Watson (Manchester United) and Peter Marinello (Arsenal) I thought we had the nucleus of a good squad but unfortunately, rather like Alex at Pittsburgh, Norm didn't have a clue and consequently we didn't get off to the best start.

To make things worse, I ended up tearing my hamstring and was told I would be out for up to 3 to 4 weeks. At this point the owner, Rick Ragone, called me in and asked me to take over the coaching role and he would keep Norm on as the GM.

This was my first official coaching role and I quickly attempted to put into practice what I had learned during my time at Pittsburgh, as well as apply the man-management skills I had seen work for John Best and Jimmy Gabriel. The lads responded great and we went onto win 11 out of the next 13 games, making the playoffs. The highlight was beating the defending champions the New York Arrows 10-6 unfortunately in the playoffs we had to play them on their home turf losing 6-5 in a very tight game.

The following season I was officially named the Head Coach and my salary was increased to $4,000 a month. The only problem was, Norm remained as GM and he and Rick were good friends from way back. It didn't take long for Norm and I to clash, he wanted to bring in a couple of players from Trinidad and Haiti, while I wanted to go with players who had played and understood the indoor game. He went ahead and signed three players, while I brought in Tommy Ord, who I knew from our time together in Seattle. I felt Tommy would be perfect to play into and off of, he was good in tight situations, scored goals and because we tried to play 2 minute shifts this would help to sharpen up his fitness levels. I knew it would take time for the new guys to settle in, but again we didn't get off to the best start, which gave Norm the chance to stick the knife in and just before Christmas I got the sack. Within a couple of days I got the job as manager of the WallBall Palace Indoor Facility which ironically was where the Inferno trained. This meant that I would still have a day to day working relationship with Sutherland as I was the one that he now had to go through if they needed to make any changes to their training schedule and I would get right up his nose when I would say I will have to take a look and will get back to you. At the end of the Inferno's second season they were taken over by a new group and moved to another training facility. We changed our name and became the Phoenix Sports Centre (PSC) we went from having 75 teams playing in various leagues to a 150 teams. I managed the indoor facility for five years and during that time I got very involved in coaching in Arizona. I also became player coach of Soko who played in both the men's indoor and outdoor leagues. I also started the Arizona State Women's Select team, before taking over the Region IV Women's team. This was another new experience for me as I visited the other states that were in my region, selecting players for the team from Washington, Colorado, Oregon, Utah, New Mexico, Hawaii and Arizona.

We went back to Washington DC to play in a tournament against the other regions, which we won and several of my squad were selected to the first Women's National Team who played in the first Women's World Cup Competition in China which they went onto win.

During my time at the PSC, I started the soccer program at Scottsdale Community College and coached there for a couple of seasons.

Through Art Becker, the Athletic Director at the college and a former pro basketball player, I was introduced to Tony Koleski, a property developer whose interest in soccer started with his daughter playing. Tony invited me to lunch one day and we talked for several hours about soccer and how nice it would be to have an outdoor professional team in Phoenix that consisted of all the best young local players.

Tony must have been impressed by what he heard, because he came back to me and said

" Lets do it! " We contacted Bill Sage, Chairman of the WSL and we were accepted for the 1989 season. I was now General Manager/Head Coach of the Arizona Condors. It was a dream job, because I had an owner who was on the same wavelength as me and was prepared to finance the whole thing.

The first season was a learning curve for the young players, but the satisfying thing was that we were not getting blown away and I could actually see some progress.

In our second season, the WSL became the APSL and although we did finish the season, Tony regrettably had to pull the plug on the Condors organization because his financial situation was hit heavily by the recession. Although we didn't win a whole lot of games, we had a really young team and I think that if we had been able to continue, we would have had the foundation of a very good team for several years.

I will always be grateful for the opportunity Tony gave me, as it was a wonderful experience.

I was approaching my 40th birthday and was very much at the crossroads. It was 1991 the NASL had folded, the MISL was in decline, I was out of work and we were in the middle of a recession. I applied for the position of Head Coach at ASU, who were looking to start a soccer program. I was interviewed for the position and I thought the interview went really well, until they told me the project was still another two years down the road. After a great deal of thought, I decided that if I wanted to stay in football I would have a better chance if I moved back to England.

In 1987, while still Manager of the PSC, working long hours seven days a week, Louis Dabo, a good friend of Portuguese stars, Eusebio and Tony Simoes and who I got to know during my playing and coaching days in the MISL, had moved to Phoenix and I invited him to be my assistant. Louis accepted my offer which afforded him the time to set up his own little soccer club for young players. He started the Santos Futbol Club and through his good friend Professor Julio Mazzei, Pele's mentor and the person responsible for bringing Pele to the US, we were invited to take a couple of teams to play in the first ever ' Pele Youth Tournament ' in Brazil. We were in São Paulo for seven nights and Rio de Janeiro for eight nights, this was an incredible experience for the kids.

Louis and I were joined by former Phoenix Inferno local boy, Mark Kerlin, who went onto have a good career in the MISL. This was also an incredible experience for the three of us and the boys did us proud. We started in São Paulo where we visited the Santos Football Club, where Pele still has his own locker in the dressing room. We went to Pele's home, which included a huge room full of the many awards he had collected over the years. One evening the kids got to meet Pele when he came to the restaurant we were eating at and I was able to share a few moments with him reflecting back on the 77 Soccer Bowl.

From São Paulo we traveled to Rio de Janeiro where our hotel was across the road from the Copacabana beach. Here, we enjoyed the Brazilian hospitality and went up Sugarloaf Mountain where we stood at the foot of the Statue of Christ the Redeemer. During our visit we spent a lot of time with Professor Mazzei and one evening we went out to dinner with him and his wife. We also met Felix the GK from that incredible 1970 Brazilian World Cup winning team.

It was truly a memorable trip and another fabulous experience I have had in what Pele describes as " The Beautiful Game "

CHAPTER EIGHT
A Catalogue of Great Memories

My list of most memorable games and times are for different reasons, but are what have made my career so very special. The first was my debut for the Sounders as a professional, away to the LA Aztecs, playing in midfield and a few weeks later, playing RB against the Vancouver Whitecaps. We lost 2-1 in LA and although it wasn't one of my better games I didn't really expect to be dropped for the home opener against Denver and it was another six games before I got a second chance. I remember being nervous, but very excited about going up against many of the players I had played with and against, during my two seasons playing for the Vancouver Spartans.

John Best had slotted me in at RB, not my preferred position, but one I had played several times during my time at Colchester United. I don't really remember to much detail about the game other than we won 2-0 and John being pleased with my performance. This was the game that opened the door for me and I went on to play another two seasons at RB.

In 77 Jimmy took over from John. We didn't get off to the best start and nine games into the season, he switched me back into midfield. I recall him pulling me in and asking how I felt about playing in the ' engine room ' again, knowing that was where I had started that very first game. He explained that he wanted to add a bit more steel in the middle of the park and he thought I was now much better equipped to do the job he had in mind. Basically, it was a holding role, where my job was to screen the back four. I was instructed to win my tackles and keep my passing game simple. I agreed to give it a shot as those are what I thought were my strengths anyways. The game was away to Dallas. We won 1-0, I got Man of the Match and Jimmy was really pleased with my performance. He kept me in midfield and we went on a terrific run to make the playoffs.

MY TOP TEN GAMES

1. June 8. 1974 Season Away to Vancouver won 2-0 my first game back in the team since the opening game of the season.

2. August 20. 1975 Season Home to Portland won 3-2 start of a fierce rivalry.

3. July 3. 1976 Season Home to Minnesota won 3-1 I scored my first goal.

4. June 2. 1977 Season Away to Dallas won 1-0 Jimmy moved me back into midfield.

5. July 18. 1977 Season Home to New York Cosmos won 1-0 and I got Pele's shirt.

6. August 4. 1977 Season Home to Hawaii won 5-0 and I opened the scoring.

7. August 21. 1977 Season Away to LA Aztecs won 3-1 in the playoffs.
   I Got Man of the Match for my Man marking job on George Best

8. May 27. 1978 Season Home to Fort Lauderdale won 3-1 it was my 99th league game and my last game before my surgery.

9. March 30. 1979 Home to Tulsa Lost 3-4 my 100th league game, I was the first player to play 100 league games for the Sounders.

10. July 21. 1979 Away to New York Cosmos we won 2-1 stopping their unbeaten run of 30 plus games.

Games against the Cosmos were always special and it was a great honour when we played against them prior to the start of the 1978 season at Giants Stadium in front of 72,000. It was billed as Franz Beckenbauer Day and the celebrities were out in numbers.

During my time with the Sounders I got to play with some top players and some great characters and we had some really good fun!

THE THREE MUSKETEERS

In 1976 I got divorced and initially I went to live with Bill and Ruth Muller, until I could find something that suited my needs. At this time Dave Gillett and Manny Matos were sharing a beautiful house over on Lake Washington, that belonged to a third guy they shared with.

One day, they went home after training to find he had put a gun inside his mouth and taken his own life. They had no idea that he wasn't coping and were shocked and upset, but both being strong characters, they knew they had to quickly put it behind them.

As I was looking for a place, we decided as a trio to start a fresh, so we rented John Best's house. Thus the " Three Musketeers were formed and the house over on Magnolia Drive became our fortress.

We got along great and in the off-season, we were the Sounders No. 1 PR team, promoting the team throughout the State. Outside of training and playing, the best times were when the season got underway and it became an ' open house ' The visiting teams used to love to come over to the after game parties. Whenever we had a party on the weekend, Manny would go around to the neighbours on both sides just to let them know it might get a little noisy. They were great, in fact the one neighbour whose house was that bit closer use to say to Manny " No problem, I'll just turn the hearing aid down "

I remember one particular party, we thought we would try and make it a bit special, so we invited all our teammates and their wives and girlfriends, in some cases both and when they arrived, we handed out flowers to all the ladies. Unfortunately, it went a bit tits up when Big Mike Ivanow showed up with three ladies he had flown in from Vegas and the team's chief scout head butted one of the guests who thought he was the DJ, when they couldn't agree on what music to play!

The ' Three Musketeers ' became two, when Dave met Linda and he started to spend more time over at her place. However this didn't slow Manny or myself down as we continued to enjoy what Seattle had to offer. I use to love going out with him, he was a babe magnet and the ladies just swarmed around him. It all became a bit of a game to him, as he would give them so much verbal that they would just give up on him and I would be there to pick up the pieces.

THE " TWO TOMMY'S "OR SHOULD I SAY THE " TWO RONNIE'S"

For those of you who do not know who the two Ronnies are, they are two British comedians, Ronnie Barker and Ronnie Corbett, who happen to be very funny and the two Tommy's are Tommy Jenkins and Tommy Ord.

I couldn't possibly make comparisons between the two pairs on the soccer field, but what I would say is both pairs made me laugh.

Both Tommy's are London boys who before coming to the states played for London clubs.

Tommy Jenks had a spell at the Orient before going to Southampton. I played with Tommy for the Sounders, Spirit and the Inferno and at each club we had some good laughs. Tommy was always much funnier when he'd had a couple of beers and I can remember one night we decided we would go for a beer. It was a bit naughty because we drove to the location. Anyways the one or two beers turned into a session and when we left the establishment we couldn't remember where we had parked the car. After almost an hour of looking we stumbled across it, as I went to put the key in the door to unlock it I dropped the keys. Simultaneously we both bent down to pick the keys up, banged heads and knocked each other on our arses.

Ordy started his career at Chelsea and I had two and a bit seasons playing with him for the Sounders and when I became Head Coach of the Inferno he was the first player I signed.

Unfortunately, it didn't all go to plan with the Inferno, however we both decided to stay in Phoenix, I got involved in coaching and Tommy got his HGV. I remember one night at the WallBall, I was just closing up when the phone rang. It was Ordy, he was on his way back from California, not to far out from Phoenix, when apparently he took a bend a little to quickly and the container on the back of his truck tipped over. I asked what was in the container and he replied cooking fat. I asked what he was going to do and quick as a flash he said " Do you fancy a fry up? " I just cracked up.

The two Tommy's in action! As I have said on a couple of occasions during the off season we did a lot of work in the schools. I remember Dave Gillett, the two Tommy's and myself going to a girls high school to do a soccer demonstration during their school assembly. When we arrived, the Main Hall was packed so we had to do it on the stage. Dave and I worked the microphone and the two Tommy's did the demo's (now you have to try to vision this) standing behind two large curtains on either side of the stage, demonstrating the push pass, driven pass and lofted pass. All you could see was the ball going back and forth at different heights. Dave and I were just cracking up and to top it all as they stepped out from behind the curtains to take a bow they received an unbelievable round of applause.

CHAPTER NINE
Catching up with Alan Hudson

Although Alan Hudson and I have a lot in common, we are, of course two very different people. One thing we do share, is that we were both captains of the Sounders and were very proud to have worn the arm band.

While Al was in England starring for Chelsea as they won the FA Cup and the European Cup Winners Cup in the early 70's, I was already in North America with my wife and young son, playing for the Vancouver Spartans, trying hard to get back into the pro game.

We came together in 1979, when he joined the Sounders for a record fee of £100,000 and we quickly hit it off.

Some of us didn't have the star-studded career that Alan had, but that didn't matter one bit to him and he treated us with friendship and respect. The feeling was mutual, so when I heard that he had fallen on hard times into his sixties, I was keen to make contact to see if I could help in any way. So, after a gap of almost 30 years and thanks to the social networking service LinkedIn, I was finally able to catch up with my former teammate.

Since then, we have met up on a few more occasions. Before he traveled back to Seattle in 2014 to celebrate the Sounders 40th Anniversary, I spoke to him about writing a book about his time in Seattle. On his return, we met up again and we talked about doing the book, but unfortunately, he had to put it on hold while he went through treatment for prostate cancer. He has since started the book and has asked me to contribute a couple of pieces.

As I began to write those pieces, the old memory juices started to flow and all of a sudden here I am writing my own book! It was not something I had planned to do. It's not like I had this incredible career in England but like Al says, everyone has a book in them and along with Dave Gillett I was the longest serving player from the original 74 squad to play for the Sounders (NASL)

Before meeting back up with Al, the only news I had heard of him in several years, apart from one or two newspaper articles, were the reports of his horrific car accident in East London in 1997, being knocked down by a car as he was crossing the road. It left him in a coma for 57 days and when he came round he found that his wife had left him. I tried to contact him when he was in the hospital, but unfortunately, no one got back to me and like a lot of people in your life, you lose touch and the time just seems to slip by.

Before the 40th Anniversary, several former Sounders players were invited to a reunion organized by Frank McDonald. Tommy Jenkins and I started to think how we might to be able to link this to doing something for Al. At this point, no contact had been made with Al himself, so I was over the moon when I was able to make contact with him through LinkedIn and I went to visit him in London. Unfortunately, we were unable to arrange anything for the reunion, but it did set the ball rolling and the next idea was the Sounders 40th Anniversary in 2014. Tommy and I got Dave Gillett involved and while they did the footwork over there, I went to see Al for the first time in almost 30 years. We arranged to meet at the Oyster Bar at the top of the escalator at the Fulham Broadway Station.

It felt just like old times. There were lots of laughs and a few tears were shed over friends no longer with us, but overall it was a lovely six hours we spent together before I had to head back home to Colchester. We discussed the Sounders 40th Anniversary and he said he would love to go back and that he would be willing to do an ' Evening with Alan Hudson, ' to offset some of the costs. My biggest fear was that we might not be able to pull it off and I didn't want to build his hopes up, only for him to be let down like he had been in the past by his former clubs Chelsea, Arsenal and Stoke. Pleasingly, through the efforts of Dave and Tommy, plus the current MLS Sounders and Alan Hinton, Al was able to go over and have a wonderful time. Disappointingly, I was unable to make the trip and I missed out on several events that had been planned.

I went to visit Al on his return and although he was not having a particularly good day, due to a bit of double vision caused by the medication he was taking for his prostate cancer, he seemed really pleased to see me and we enjoyed our meet. It was the first chance to chat since he returned from his visit to Seattle and he told me how honoured he felt to be named the Sounders Best Ever Player and to be selected to the Sounders all-time top team. They also named a second X1 all-time team and I too was honoured to be included.

NASL Sounders All – Time Eleven

Gk Tony Chursky

D Ray Evans **D** Dave Gillett **D** Mike England **D** Jeff Stock

M Jimmy Gabriel **M** Alan Hudson **M** Steve Buttle **M** Bruce Rioch

F Jimmy Robertson **F** Roger Davies **F** Tommy Hutchinson

NASL Sounders 2nd X1

Gk Jack Brand

D Mel Machin **D** Ian Bridge **D** David Nish **D** Jimmy McAlister

M Adrian Webster **M** Arfon Griffiths **M** Harry Redknapp

F Peter Ward **F** John Rowland's **F** Micky Cave **F** Mark Peterson **F** Gordon Wallace

Like many of his Sounders teammates, I feel very privileged to have played alongside Alan Hudson. He is a bit like Marmite, you either love it or you hate it and I personally love it!

As a player, his record speaks for itself. What I saw when Al landed in Seattle, was someone who loved his football and equally loved to train. He started his career at Chelsea and experienced much success very early and with that success came a superstar image as he played alongside the likes of Osgood and Cooke and socialized with the late great George Best. He even had Besties good looks and charisma and did some modeling. Some even referred to him as London's answer to Best.

In making comparisons to the modern day players, I

have no doubt the likes of Pele, Best and Hudson, would have still been outstanding players today. You have to remember we live in a different society today and football is very different. In our day, there was a drinking culture in the game whereby players socialized with the fans who had worked all week to pay for their tickets and liked to let their hair down on the weekends. Al and George were particularly high-profile players and because of their celebrity status, they were judged not just on their performance, but also on how much alcohol they had consumed and which ' dolly bird ' they were going home with. The media had a field day!

I mention all this because when Best and Hudson came over to the US, a lot of questions were asked over whether they could still perform at the high level they had shown during their careers in England. George was first to arrive and I have to say how delighted I was to get to play against him on several occasions. There was no doubt in any bodies mind that George meant business as he got himself in great shape and for the first couple of seasons showed the NASL why he was regarded as world class. Al's arrival a couple of seasons later was a big boost for the Sounders as all the clubs were starting to bring the big names over, including the Cosmos, who signed Beckenbauer and Carlos Alberto.

Al was only capped twice for England so coming to the States enabled him to match his footballing abilities against some of the worlds greats who had joined the NASL. What I loved about Al when he arrived was there was no ' Billy Big Time ' attitude, he just went about trying to get the best out of his teammates.

One thing I have learned in my life, is you don't always have control over your destiny and that certainly seems to be the case with Al. What I would say to those that feel Al has a chip on his shoulder is that you have to have played in his boots to know where he is coming from. To have had it all and then have it taken away by someone who has no idea about the game and later to be mowed down by a car leaving you in a coma for 57 days and then to be diagnosed with prostate cancer... wouldn't you feel a bit hard done by? Al loves his football and has an opinion on many things, some things make him frustrated. He hates to see modern day players underachieving and the hierarchy getting richer by dictating the direction of football in our country.

I am sure we have all asked the question, ' what if ' many times. I believe that if Al and Alan Hinton hadn't have been shafted in Seattle by certain individuals Al would have stayed and got involved in coaching and I am sure he would have been as big of a success as in his playing days. Sometimes things happen for a reason and maybe Al still has a part to play, or like the late, Great, Bobby Moore, will all that wealth and knowledge go to waste?

It was nice to see how well the new generation of Sounders fans showed their appreciation of Al's contribution to soccer in Seattle and the US, when he attended the Sounders Vs Whitecaps game, where he received the Golden Scarf. The fans in Seattle have always played an important part in the Sounders history and it doesn't surprise me one bit that they are in the top 10 of the World rankings for the highest average attendance. Seattle has always been a soccer hotbed and it is great that so many of the former Sounders players have stayed in the area and have gotten involved in putting something back into the community.

A few years ago, along with Al, I was very proud to be named to the fans favourite All-Time Sounders team. The votes came out as follows, in a 4 – 4 – 2 formation

Hahnemann

Webster, England, Jenkins (S), Jackson

Hudson, Gabriel, Buttle, Farrell

Davies Fry

As I have said, there are still many former Sounders players who have made Seattle there home Jimmy Gabriel, Bobby Howe, Dave Gillett, Tommy Jenkins, Tony Chursky, Frank Barton and Ray Evans. Not a bad team!

However there is one former player who came through the system who I think has done a tremendous job in helping the young soccer players in the State of Washington to develop and to progress and that is Jimmy McAlister.

JIMMY MAC

Although most teams in the NASL were made up of mostly foreign players, the first local boy to break into the Sounders lineup was Jimmy McAlister.

In 1977, he was an integral part of the team's success in reaching the Soccer Bowl Final. Not only did he go on to have a very good career himself, but he also opened the door for the likes of Jeff Stock, Mark Peterson,

ADRIAN WEBSTER

Eddie Krueger and Bernie James to follow.

I do believe Jimmy had a good grounding playing in the reserves under Harry Redknapp and then having Head Coach Jimmy Gabriel give him his opportunity to play in the first team at such a young age was quite an accomplishment.

Although naturally right footed, he was slotted in at LB and he went onto make that his position. I think Jimmy's strengths were he had good speed endurance and could get up and down the park. He was comfortable on the ball and for a young lad he had a good understanding of his position. I think his game certainly benefited from playing in a back four that included the very experienced Machin, Gillett and England.

What I liked about Jimmy, was that he never let any of his success go to his head and he continued to work hard to develop his game and he always had the upmost respect for his coaches and teammates.

He was a bit of a cheeky chappie (I think he must have got that from Harry) and had no problems in dealing with the dressing room banter!

I don't know if he realised at the time, but he had become a role model for all the young local kids that could now see a pathway into professional soccer.

Like many of his teammates in 1979, he went to play in the MISL for the Buffalo Stallions for one season before returning to the NASL where he played for

180

Toronto and San Jose. It was inevitable that he would return to the State of Washington and he finished his playing career in the MISL with the Tacoma Stars, playing alongside many of his former teammates

It is testament to his character, that when he finished playing, he wanted to put something back into the game and he is now Director of Coaching for Seattle United Youth.

I think Jimmy Mac has earned the title of ' Mr. Soccer ' in the State of Washington, for his contribution to both the pro game and the development of youth soccer.

ADRIAN WEBSTER

CHAPTER TEN
The End of an Era

As I queued for the plane at the Phoenix Sky Harbour International Airport on Saturday, November 2 1991, I had no idea what direction my life was about to take. My 40th birthday was just four days away. I no longer had a full-time job and it seemed like my 17- plus years in the US were over. I was comforted by the thought that if things didn't work out back home in England, I still held a ' green card ' and could flee back into the arms of Uncle Sam again!

November 1991 was certainly a watershed month, in all sorts of ways. It was the month Freddie Mercury died of AIDS, the month Robert Maxwell fell off his yacht and drowned and the month Russian President Boris Yeltsin outlawed the Communist Party. My own situation didn't make such big headlines, but to me, this was still very much the dawn of a new era.

I had purchased a one-way ticket back to England and had put all my household belongings into storage. I flew from Phoenix to Los Angeles, to catch my connecting flight and at LA I had to transfer my luggage. Just as I bent down to pick up my large kit bag, another hand reached forward to pick up the same bag. I lifted my head to see the hand belonged to none other than the Scottish comedian, Billy Connolly, who was on the same flight and was scheduled to perform in LA . We quickly resolved the problem as it was ' Webster ' not ' Connolly ' whose name was on the tag we turned over! We wished each other good luck as we headed off in different directions.

It was a long flight home and I remember sitting on the plane, knocking back a few Brandy and lemonades and using the time to reflect back on some of the great times I had. I also wondered if I was making the right decision and what the future might have in store for me, now that my forties beckoned. I was met at Heathrow Airport by my sister, Pauline and her husband Kevin and by the time we got to Colchester, I must admit I was still having doubts. It had been a couple of years since I was last home and I don't know what it was, but everything seemed so much smaller, especially later on at my mum and dad's house when I climbed into a single bed, having been use to sleeping in a King-sized waterbed!

My biggest fear of all, was what I was going to do for a living and I remember saying to my mum, " I guess I had better get a proper job, " to which she just smiled. After spending a couple of days acclimatizing, I just had one thing on my mind and that was to celebrate my 40th birthday. After a few beers in my local pub, I got a taxi to one of my old haunts, the Windmill Night Club, where I had spent many Saturday nights with my mates. During the evening, I was introduced to this guy who seemed to be having as much fun as I was so we shared a couple of drinks and I was pleased to make the acquaintance of the Colchester United manager, Roy

McDonough.

Things seemed to move quickly and by the end of November, I had taken over from the former Colchester and Wrexham player, Steve Dowman, as manager of Brightlingsea United, who played in the Jewson Premier League. They were bottom of the league and I had no idea about the local scene, but it was a start, so ' in for a penny, in for a pound. '

I was confident in my ability to coach and thought this job might open a few doors for me.

At the time I was having problems with my shoulder, so I enquired if I could get an appointment to see Doctor Peter Snell who had been the club Doctor at Colchester United when I was there. This brought me into contact with two people that have been very important to me over the years. The first was Terry Price, a former teammate at Colchester, who I went to see after my shoulder had cleared up, as he now had his own gym over at the Arena close by to where I was living. He helped me with my rehab and got me into weight training. More than 20 years later I am still training there 3 times a week. Over the years I have had back surgery, a hip replacement and my two big toes fused and pinned and each time Terry has helped with my rehab. The other person I came into contact with was my now wife Jo. She is not a big football fan, but she has supported me all the way even when it was seven days a week and she was holding down a full-time job as a receptionist at the doctors surgery.

Colchester is a growing town, but when it comes to football, it is still a relatively small place and getting the Brightlingsea job helped to reacquaint me with a lot of old football friends as well as develop a new generation of contacts. One of the first people I came back into contact with was Steve Foley, the youth team manager at Colchester. Steve and I had played together in the youth and reserve team's at Layer Road and after I left to go to Canada Steve went onto play over 300 games for the first team. Steve said he was happy for me to go along to some of his training sessions and on several occasions he asked me to put on a session for the kids and sometimes when he needed an extra body I would join in.

I talked to Steve about setting up a Summer Soccer Camp, which he liked the idea of and said he would run it by the Manager Roy McDonough and the Chairman Gordon Parker. A few days later he came back to me to say the club had agreed to it. So in August 1992, I ran the first Colchester United Summer Soccer Camp at

Essex University supported by Roy and the Colchester United players. We had 110 kids attend the weeklong event and the feedback we got was very positive.

Before the camp, I was working hard to keep Brightlingsea in the top division of the Jewson League on a budget of £120 a week, of which I got £40 and some expenses, all of which came out of the Chairmans pocket. Mourinho eat your heart out!

Through Steve giving me a few coaching jobs he was not able to do himself I was picking up another £100 – 150 a week, so things were starting to look up and offers started to come my way. The lads at Brightlingsea were terrific and although the money was rubbish, they were happy to put what they got and a few quid more back behind the bar after the game. We had a really good team spirit, stuck together and avoided relegation by finishing third from bottom above their arch rivals Clacton Town. At the end of the season, the club asked me to stay on for the following season. I was happy to do so and asked for £60 a week to do it, which they turned down, so I moved on and got the manager's job at Halstead Town, another Jewson League outfit in Essex.

During my time at Brightlingsea, I learned that the players followed the money, so when I went to Halstead a lot of people said I was taking a step up and that there were some very good players over at Rosemary Lane. However what my new Chairman neglected to tell me was that all the better players had moved on! When I went over to start pre-season, I could tell I had my work cut out and with the budget I was given to work with it was always going to be difficult to replace the quality that had moved on. Although the lads worked hard in training, in the games we were simply not good enough, so just before Christmas, I parted company with the club.

After Christmas, I continued to do some coaching for several clubs in the Colchester and District Youth League and concentrated my efforts on organizing a second Summer Camp.

Jo and I were now living together and while doing the coaching, which was mostly in the evenings, I applied for several jobs outside of football. Although I loved my football, there were times I had no money coming in because during the winter months the weather was not always conducive so if I didn't coach I didn't get paid.

The second camp was another big success, this time we attracted 120 youngsters and were able to do a bit more through some sponsorship we got and the T-Shirts the kids received was great advertising for future camps. Through the success of the camps I was offered a full-time position working in the Club Shop at Layer Road.

CHAPTER ELEVEN
Back Where it all Started

And so, in September 1993, I found myself back at Colchester United in full-time employment, 25 years after first joining them as an apprentice professional when leaving school. The money wasn't great - £125 a week – but it was a regular pay cheque, which was the most important thing, as it had been a while. It also meant I now had my foot back in the door to the pro game!

Working in the Club Shop meant I met many of the supporters and on match days, I got to see a good part of the first team games. By then I had gotten to know the Player/Manager, Roy McDonough and it was an exciting time at the club as he guided the team to the Conference FA Trophy and promotion back into the Football League. He was a colorful character who built a fearsome reputation on the number of red cards he received. Hence, the " *Red Card Roy* " title of his successful autobiography, published several years later.

Steve Foley would often come into the shop in the afternoons and we would spend hours talking football, especially about youth development. I mentioned to him how I thought it would be great if the club could put an AstroTurf in behind the bar-side stand, which is where as youth players we had spent many hours playing head-tennis. Tony Willoughby and his Sporting Chances organization had moved out and I had a bunch of ideas on how we could utilize the area. Steve went to speak to the hierarchy who looked into available funding. Around about this time, former Colchester United Legend, Micky Cook, had returned to the club as the Football in the Community Officer and through his organization, we were able to get the funding to put in the AstroTurf, boards and floodlights and I went from running the Club Shop, to Soccer Centre Manager and I started the Soccer Kids program.

Steve was always looking at how he could improve the youth setup at the club and in conjunction with the Soccer Centre, he wanted to increase the number of teams from just the U18's to include U16, U15 and U14's. Steve had an old school friend of mine, Steve Dale, running the U16's but he thought it made more sense, now that I was full-time at the club, if I took over the U16's and he brought in Neil Partner to take the U15's and Geoff Harrop to take the U14's.

The Soccer Kids program I started, proved to be a good recruiting tool for the young local players. I first met Geoff when he returned to England from Australia about the same time as I came back from the US. Former Colchester United CF, Roy Massey, was now a PE teacher at my old school Thomas Lord Audley (known as Monkwick Secondary in my day) and he asked Geoff and me to do some coaching at the school and from there we also worked together doing some sessions that Steve set up over at Maldon.

Roy was sacked in 1994, to be succeeded by George Burley, who left after 20 games, to take over the Ipswich Town job, where he went onto have considerable success. The next manager through the door was Steve Wignall, a former player at the club. This didn't go down to well with youth team coach Steve Foley as he had been caretaker manager on a couple of occasions and now when he thought he was ready to take the job on, the board of directors overlooked him. Steve left to join his former teammate Micky Walker at Norwich City and was there for 10 year's as reserve team manager and first team coach.

By now I had been the Soccer Centre Manager for four years, during which time I had worked with over 750 kids, working Mon. to Fri. 4:30 pm to 9:30 pm and on Saturdays I did Birthday parties and Match Day tours of the ground and on Sundays I managed the U16 team. A pretty full schedule and I worked my socks off, so when Steve moved on I thought I would apply for the position. Steve Wignall gave me an interview, but informed me that he had given the job to Micky Cook who had been his teammate when they played together at the club. Obviously, I was disappointed, but he said he had plans for the youth set-up and he wanted to get me involved.

So Micky came in as Head of Youth and several changes were made in accordance with the new guidelines set down by the Football League. Substantial funding was made available and Geoff Harrop became the Centre of Excellence Manager, I became the Recruitment Officer and Katy Springett the Youth Secretary. Micky's job was to oversee and report back to club director, Peter Powell, on all aspects of the youth department as well as on the development of the youth team that he coached. We went from running U14-16 to U9-16 teams and Geoff was responsible for bringing in the coaches for each age group and implementing the coaching curriculum put together by Micky. My role was to try to get the best local kids into the program and develop a scouting network. We were all given four year contracts, which was great because we had all been involved in youth development and knew that it was an investment in time and didn't just happen overnight.

Steve Bradshaw and Steve Downey took over the Football in the Community project, the Soccer Centre and the Soccer Kids programs that Micky and I had set up. A portakabin was set up at the ground and Katy ran the day to day stuff and Andy Hunt became the Youth Team Physio. The Centre of Excellence was set up over at Essex University and Geoff put together a really good team of coaches and Micky asked me to continue with the U16's. The C of E games were played on Sundays, which was Micky's day off however he trusted Geoff and I to oversee the running of it.

The guidelines for recruiting kids U9-12 were they had to live within a one hour radius and kids U13-16 an hour and a half. The philosophy of the club was to provide a pathway for the kids to develop and progress and the coaches were encouraged to do all the new coaching qualifications that were being introduced by the FA.

At U16 Micky would start to invite the better players in to work with the current scholars, this is where Geoff and I would have a big input and it gave Micky the chance to take a good look at them in the environment they would be entering. It was then down to Micky to produce players for the first team. When everything was put into place Chairman Gordon Parker pulled me to one side and said that as part of my role, he wanted me to respond to all the trial letters the club received, which I did and this is how we got Greg Halford, Gary Richards and Anthony Wordsworth, who all went onto play pro and were later sold bringing into the club approx. £2,500,000

Geoff was great at fund raising and through his efforts we were able to make sure the kids got the best that we could give them. I guess ultimately how you are judged is by the number of kids that turn pro and make the first team. Over the years, we produced the likes of Lomano Tresor Lua Lua, Greg Halford, Dean Morgan, Dean Gerken, John White, Gary Richards, Anthony Wordsworth, Mark Cousins and Medi Elito.

Two players that I thought were very unlucky not to get

pro we're Liam Coleman and Angelo Harrop, who were not the biggest, but technically and tactically were very good. I think had they been Spanish I have no doubt they would have got pro!

After a successful period under Steve Wignall, who took them to two Wembley appearances, promotion via the playoffs and the Associates Members Cup Final, things changed after he resigned in January 1999. He was replaced by Mick Wadsworth, a well respected FA coach, who kept Steve Whitton on as his assistant. In his short spell in charge, I think Wadsworth upset a few people, but I personally got on well with him. My first meeting with him, he asked me who we're the recruitment officers at three different clubs, which I didn't know, but I soon understood where he was coming from and in my role as Recruitment Officer, he gave me the responsibility of setting up trials on a regular basis for him to look at players that were available. He also invited me into all of his Friday afternoon meetings with ' Whitts ' and allowed me to have an input. He was quite an intimidating character and I think the board eventually felt he was a bit to overpowering and they released him from his duties.

Steve Whitton took over as manager and he made Geraint Williams his number two. Whitts was a very experienced player, who started his career with Coventry, he also played for WestHam and Ipswich before moving to Colchester. I had gotten to know him through helping Micky with the Youth team, so when he took over, I went to see him and asked what it was he looked for in a player. He basically said ' two things ' players that are comfortable receiving the ball and can pass it! This was very much along the lines of my philosophy of control, pass and move and has been the foundation of how I coach.

He wasn't really into the youth, so I was a bit surprised when he took a liking to Dean Morgan and gave him a pro contract. Unfortunately, I don't think Dean really made the best of his opportunity and in my opinion has never really fulfilled his potential. Outside of Lomano I think Dean was the best young player I had worked with during my 13 years of working in the youth setup at the club. As part of the Kids development at the C of E, we had to keep a log of their games, write a short appraisal of their performance and give them a mark out of 10, as part of their feedback. Deans marks were consistently 8 and 9 and he scored goals regularly, two or three per game.

Under Steve, the first team played some nice football. However, he subsequently left by mutual agreement in 2003 and as far as I know, has dropped out of football. Next through the revolving door, was Phil Parkinson, who I think was the best manager during my time at the club. He took an interest in all aspects of the club, from the Football in the Community, up to the first team, he certainly put the hours in. His backroom staff consisted of Geraint Williams, Brian Owen, Paul Dyer (chief scout) and Stuart Aylesbury (physio and fitness coach) and he utilized each ones many strengths. Phil made over 500 league appearances and Colchester was his first managerial position. He was well organized, very passionate, a good motivator and he lead the team to promotion to the Championship, for the very first time in the 2005-06 season.

Geoff Harrop left to take up a similar position with Rushden & Diamonds and my role now became the Youth Development Officer, which meant I was still in charge of recruiting but was now also the C of E Manager. Phil would often come over to our training nights and to the games on a Sunday morning and would ask me who were the good young players coming through. He liked Greg Halford right away and it wasn't long before Greg made his senior debut. Another was Gary Richards, who before making his debut, was nearly sent out on loan, but was suddenly needed for a first team game that was also being televised and he ended up being ' Man of the Match ' Both Greg and Gary were players I had invited in after getting letters asking for a trial and were then brought in for a six-week trial before I signed them.

Phil, was unfortunately caught up in the dismissal of Micky Cook, but to be fair, his hands were tied and the decision came from higher up. Phil was left saying he was sorry about it, for he didn't personally have a problem with Micky, but he needed to concentrate on the first team.

Phil had a great work ethic and he got his rewards in the 2005-06 season when the team finished second to gain automatic promotion to the Championship. It was the club's first time at this level, 70 years after turning professional just before the Second World War.

However, Phil decided to resign in June 2006 to become the new manager of Hull City.

When Micky left, I was very disappointed not to get the

chance to coach the youth team, as I felt I had paid my dues and was ready to give it a go. I was called into the office by Marie Partner, who was now the Chief Executive and was told that the Chairman Peter Heard had given the job to Joe Dunne and that they would like me to work closely with him. Although disappointed I was pleased for Joe, as I had gotten to know him as a player and when he brought his nephew who was over from Ireland to a couple of my Soccer Kids sessions.

As a player what Joe lacked in ability, he more than made up for with a tremendous determination. He wore his heart on his sleeve and was a very loyal club man and a favourite with the fans. Joe had the same work ethic as Phil and demanded the same from the kids that played for him.

To be Head of Youth, you need to have your UEFA 'A' license and I have never seen anyone go through all the courses as quickly as Joe did to secure his position. When Micky was Head of Youth, I would go over to the University of Essex with him a couple of mornings a week to help him with the coaching, but for some reason Joe preferred to do it all himself, so I just concentrated and put all my energy into the C of E which was fine with me.

My job had now become seven days week: Mon-Fri. 9:00 am to 4:00 pm in the office, Monday 6:00 – 7:30 pm U16's training, Wednesday 6:00 – 9:00 pm C of E training,

Friday 6:00 – 7:30 pm C of E training, Saturday U16 game, Sunday 9:00 – 2:00 pm C of E games.

As you can see, a busy schedule and very little time for scouting. However, 1 was lucky in that I had put together a good scouting team who were Colchester through and through.

Joe would quite often do a bit of scouting for Phil and when ever I could I would tag along with him. On a couple of occasions, we bumped into John Gorman, who Joe knew from his Gillingham days and I knew from our time together in Phoenix.

What I liked about Joe was that he didn't suffer fools gladly and he would let them know if need be! I think in his early years, he was a bit impatient as a coach and if it didn't work straight away, he would get very frustrated and quickly start making changes. Under John Ward, he showed a lot more patience and didn't seem to get so uptight and I found him to be much more relaxed.

Joe got off to a great start in his first season as Youth Team Coach and had a terrific FA Cup run, beating Cardiff, Crewe and Chelsea (coached by Brendan Rogers) before going out in the sixth round. I was on the bench with him for the Crewe and Chelsea games and on both nights, he got his tactics spot on. I enjoyed my time working with both Micky and Joe, whose personalities and coaching styles were very different, but what I would say is that they were both Colchester United through and through.

During my time back at Colchester United, there were certainly some memorable occasions.

The Wembley trips come instantly to mind, the first being the FA Trophy Final in 1992, traveling up on the same coach as Perry Groves and then seeing our young youth product, Karl Duguid, play in Steve Wignall's side. It was also great to go to Stamford Bridge and watch young John White play on Phil Parkinson's team against the mighty Chelsea in the FA Cup.

However, some of the best fun was getting the boots back on to play for the Colchester United Vets team, which included my former teammates Micky Cook, Steve Foley, Steve Leslie and Phil Bloss as well as several other players that came after my time, including Steve Wignall, Paul Dyer, Steve Dowman, Micky Packer, Dennis Longhorn and Ian Allison.

We entered the Umbro Cup competition which had its final at Wembley- the rules were you had to be over 35, I think most of us were over 40. We managed to beat Leyton Orient and Aldershot, before going out to a youthful Blackburn Rovers side, who had guys that were still playing in the Conference League. We were 4-0 down in the first 20 minutes, but came back to finally lose 7-4. I remember it being a very physical game and Micky Cook having to go off to the hospital with one of the biggest bruises I had ever seen! I also got to play on Rod Stewart's pitch at his home in Epping, along with a few other ex Col.Utd players like Phil Coleman, Steve Wright, Geoff Harrop, Ian Phillips and Jeff Wood and then go onto spend a lovely afternoon with him and his wife, Penny, at his local pub.

Being in a clubs youth setup, is always nice when the

kids do well and what bigger stage than the prestigious FA Youth Cup! I remember going to Villa Park with Steve Foley and his team and I'm sure the kids that were involved still have great memories of playing against Aston Villa. I stood in for Steve the following season at Portman Road against Ipswich, when a late equalizer for Ipswich gave them another chance and we lost the replay at Layer Road. Micky also had some very good Cup runs taking us to Ewood Park, Blackburn, Elland Road, Leeds and to Highbury Stadium home of the famous Arsenal.

CHAPTER TWELVE
A Time to Re – assess

There came a point where the 7 days a week schedule was beginning to take its toll. I was having problems with my back, which stemmed from an injury I sustained when moving a heavy fence curb they had left in the pathway at the Soccer Centre when installing the Astro Turf. I was 55 by then and starting to think maybe I needed to take a step back. Micky, after a short spell away from the game was asked to set up a Football Academy over at the Colne Community College in Brightlingsea and he asked me to join them for their second season. I told Micky I would talk it through with my wife Jo and get back to him. Under the circumstances, we thought it was an offer I couldn't turn down. The timetable was Monday to Friday with no weekend duties, three mornings were coaching in schools and four afternoons coaching the college second string with games on Wednesday afternoons, plus 13 weeks paid holidays. The first person at Colchester United I let know was Joe Dunne, who said he understood, but asked me to go away and think about it. My mind was made up and I let Micky know I was up for it.

It was during the 2006 pre-season, when I gave my

notice to the club. Phil Parkinson had moved on Geraint Williams was the new manager. I liked ' George ' he had a nice manner and was the kind of manager I would have liked to have played for. On the day of the pre-season photo-call the Chairman Peter Heard strolled over and said " I don't suppose you would change your mind " I politely said no and he thanked me for my efforts and wished me good luck. It kind of felt like I had been here before! By the day that I left came around I had got wind that a certain individual at the club couldn't be arsed to get everyone together to say there goodbyes, which was the norm when somebody had been at the club a lengthy time and was leaving. This I found very disappointing, but then it just showed Marie Partners true colours and just reinforced what most people at the club thought, that she was a two-faced bitch!

Anyways, I was able to go around and say my farewells to the rest of the staff who I got along really well with. Everyone wished me good luck and Joe presented me with a lovely leather travel and wash bag and I think the club threw in an empty Colchester United wallet.

I think the hardest thing for me, was saying goodbye to all the kids, parents and everyone I worked with at the C of E – people like Brian Swift, Phil Eley and Danny King. It was quite overwhelming, as I received some lovely gifts and good wishes for my new job.

I was 13 years back at the club and as I drove home from the University I felt a sense of pride knowing I had served the club well.

I started at the Colne College in September 2006, where I linked up with former Millwall and Colchester United player, Phil Coleman, who was now the Head of PE there. I first got to know Phil when he brought his son Liam to one of my Soccer Kids sessions and I knew straight away this kid was going to be a good player. Later on Geoff Harrop got Phil involved at the C o E. We also played in some Vets games together and although I had never seen Phil play before, you could tell that he would have been a handful to play against. He was a tough rugged type of player, a great header of the ball and very competitive. Micky was the Director of Football, Jon Taylor the Director of Sport and my new role was Assistant Director of Football. Jon had played in the same youth team as Jamie Redknapp at Bournemouth and is a UEFA ' A ' licensed coach, who worked alongside Bryan Klug at the Ipswich Town Youth Academy.

Micky also brought in a very good friend of ours, Brian Swift a UEFA ' B ' coach and now a Sports Injury Therapist and a FA Medical Tutor. Brian had also been the reserve team manager at Darlington in the 1980's' under Cyril Knowles, the well-known Tottenham fullback.

The program at the Colne is into its tenth season as I write this and I think we have developed a highly respected academy. I feel it has benefited from my years of recruitment and I still have a handle on the local scene as I also scout for Ipswich Town Youth Academy.

Steve McGavin is the Head of Recruitment and Welfare

and he asked me to do some scouting after I bumped into him in Colchester one day when I was parking my car. Steve was a skillful forward who was sold to Birmingham City by Colchester for £150,000 he then moved to Wycombe for £175,000 before returning to Colchester for a second spell.

The Colne currently runs three teams, of which two play in the Conference Youth Alliance, in different divisions and our third team plays in the Essex College First Division. When I was a kid growing up in Colchester, there were no Sunday leagues; football was very big in the schools and if you were good enough you were selected for your District and County teams, in my case Colchester and Essex. The boys that I now coach, are 16-18 year olds, who do their education in the mornings and football in the afternoons. Having coached thousands of kids over the years, this is the age group I prefer to work with. You can have a bit of banter with them, but when it comes to training and playing they know I mean business. As part of their development, Jon organizes a tour every year, normally to Spain. We have been to Valencia, Real Madrid twice, where we stayed at the Spanish Federation Sports Complex and in 2015 it was our second visit to Barcelona. Not only is this a great football experience for the boys, it is a cultural education as we try to expose them to as many opportunities as possible.

When I first returned from the US in 1991 and coached at Brightlingsea and Halstead, there were very few young players playing Senior football. Today, if you look at the makeup of the local team's, things have changed tremendously. I think the Colne has played a big part in developing and preparing these young players to make that step up from youth football to senior football and teams such as AFC Sudbury, Brightlingsea, Wivenhoe, Stanway Rovers and Clacton are reaping the benefits.

At professional clubs, they have to make decisions on boys at 16, in regards to whether they are going to offer them a scholarship or not. At 16 there are many that are not physically ready, but at colleges like the Colne, we can give them a couple of more years to develop, as well as provide further education. Most of the boys that come to the Colne, do the BTech Sports Diploma which is the equivalent to three ' A ' levels and can get them into University. Last year, we got our first boy back into the pro game – Aidan Austin was released at 16 by Norwich City, he came to us and with in months, was invited to the Nike Academy and eventually was given a pro contract at Nottingham Forest.

I don't think anything ever replaces the enjoyment and satisfaction of playing the game, but the pleasure I now get is to see these young players progress, whether it be in college, senior or pro football. I also think along with hard work there has to be an element of luck and being in the right place at the right time and I can now look back with great satisfaction knowing I played apart in helping many young boys progress in the game.

ADRIAN WEBSTER

CHAPTER (Unlucky for some) THIRTEEN
Contemplating Half - a - Century in Football

As I write this, I am approaching the grand old age of 65 and unless I suddenly get the England job, I will probably retire from the Colne soon. I think 49 years of having been involved in football since I left school is long enough and hopefully, it will give me a bit more time to go and watch my grandsons play.

When I first went to Canada and then onto bigger and better things in the US, I never dreamed I would finish my footballing days back here in Colchester. But there are no regrets, it has just been part of my journey. When I got back involved in football locally in my hometown of Colchester, I met Pete Newman and Peter Andrews who are both heavily involved with the Colchester and District Youth League and who work there socks off to give young kids a good start in the game and for that I take my hat off to them and to all the other people involved who give up so much of their time and energy to make it work.

As I contemplate retirement from football, I hope I can be forgiven for drifting back to those balmy Sounders days thinking about the great players and characters with whom I shared so many wonderful seasons in the sun. Both Alan Hudson and I ultimately left Seattle in less than ideal circumstances and both of us would have loved to have ended up coaching the Sounders once our playing days were over. Perhaps even doing it together! Why not? We were both captains at the club and hugely enjoyed our time there and both feel we would have had a lot to offer. I know one thing for sure, it would have been fun!

Now I have reached this stage I would like to select my all time Sounders team from the players I played with. Using my coaching head I have selected the following players in a

3 - 4 – 3 system.

GK Tony Chursky

D Dave Gillett **D** Mike England **D** Jimmy Gabriel

M Jimmy Robertson **M** Alan Hudson **M** Steve Buttle **M** Tommy Jenkins

F Micky Cave **F** Tommy Ord **F** Derek Smethurst

My system gives me three diamonds and good team shape and balance. My style of play would be to encourage a control, pass and move strategy as well as to give the more flair players in the team a license to express themselves. The key is to be positive and to move the ball quickly. My three at the back are all good solid defenders who are also comfortable on the ball, have a good range of passing and can play out from the back. My four in midfield include Robertson who can play wide on both sides and Jenkins who could work a rotation with Buttle as well as provide us with width when we have possession of the ball. Both Robertson and Jenkins are a threat when running at defenders. I would also expect my wide players to provide us with good crosses into the box, as well as track back when necessary. By making Hudson my skipper, I think it would bring the best out of him and his role would be to dictate the tempo of the game and to keep looking to make those forward runs. Buttle's role would be to get on the ball and to use that magic wand to provide those pinpoint passes to open up the opposition. Cave and Smethurst would be required to play in between the FB and CB on either side, as well as to get into the box to attack crosses coming in. Movement is very important, as it asks questions of defenders. Ord would play through the middle as our target man – someone we could play into and off of and I would be looking at 15-20 goals a season from him. Our three forwards would also have defensive responsibilities and that would be firstly to drop off, to encourage them to play out from the back

and then as a unit quickly apply pressure. This affords

our midfield and defenders to retain good shape and balance. If this was not working, I would go to plan B which would be to overload the midfield by withdrawing a forward switching to a 3 – 5 – 2 formation. I might have to go to the bench and bring Webster on in a holding midfield role.

So there you have it. What a team! The strength is that we have some good strong characters that are comfortable on the ball and are all good decision makers. I think my choices would have certainly entertained the fans and I know for one I would have paid to watch them!

THE FINAL CHAPTER

The Golden Scarf

Catching up with Dave Gillett, Jimmy McAlister with grandson, Dave Butler, Jeff Stock, Alan Hinton, AW

and Dave D'Errico.

Adrian Webster and Wade Webber before March to the Match

Adrian and Claudia Best, wife of the first Sounders Coach John Best.

Dave Butler, team owner, Adrian Hanauer, and Adrian

Dave Butler, Adrian, Jenni and Bill Conner, Dave and Linda.

The three originals Butler, Gillett, and Webster!

Adrian, the owner of Fuel, Mike Morris, Dave Gillett and Dave Butler at a fan meet and greet before the game.

Memorial Stadium with Jimmy Gabriel, Adrian, and Dave Gillett.

Adrian having lunch with Jimmy and Pat Gabriel.

As I started to write the final chapter I took a moment to reflect on the last couple of years. Shortly after completing my first book Eternal Blue Forever Green I had surgery for bowel cancer and after the surgery it was my goal to get through the rehab and to return to working at the College where I coached. At the end of the season I was only a few months away from my 65th birthday, so I thought that this would be a good time to take my retirement. I felt I needed a break from football and there were a couple of trips I wanted to take. Because I had missed the Sounders 40th Anniversary, a trip back to Seattle was high on my list.

In talking with Jenni Conner the publisher of my two books we felt that it would be good to tie the visit in with trying to promote the books. Jenni and her husband Bill were planning a trip over to England so in May 2017 my wife Jo and I met up with them in London where we spent an enjoyable three days. While there we put the final pieces of the commemorative book 40th Anniversary Soccer Bowl 77 Seattle Sounders Vs New York Cosmos (which are both available on Amazon) together with a view to bringing it out a month before I went over.

Outside of Jenni my only other contacts that were soccer and Sounders related were David Falk of goalWA.net and Frank MacDonald of the " Washington State Legends of Soccer " whom I had been interviewed by in regards to my time in Seattle as a Sounders player.

The last time I was in Seattle was 26 years ago when I had traveled from Phoenix to do my USSF ' B ' License and I stayed with my former teammate and good friend Dave Gillett.

During my 26 years back in England I was lucky to stay involved in soccer, I had 13 years back at my first club Colchester United working in youth development and then 10 years at the College coaching 16-18 years old students.

I think the soccer wear and tare has taken it's toll over the years, having had a back operation, a hip replacement and both my big toes pinned and fused. I don't think anything ever replaces playing, however I do think that having worked mostly in youth development it has given me a great deal of satisfaction.

I am not one to say if I had it all to do over again I would do it the same way because for me that says you didn't make to many mistakes and I know I certainly made a few.

Regrets: I think it would have been nice to have had a more successful playing career in my home town of Colchester, but then I would not have experienced the wonderful times I had in Canada and the US.

Leaving the Sounders as I did, I think I should have said to Jack Daley I will go to Pittsburgh for the season, because I needed to get back to playing regular and I will then come back and take my chances under Alan Hinton.

I guess the downside to my long involvement in soccer is that I didn't spend the time I would have liked to with my kids and now because of the distance I am missing out on the grandchildren growing up!

In Phoenix I got into coaching through being injured and although I jumped at the opportunity, with hindsight I think it would have been much better for me to have first been a number two. However coaching in Phoenix at youth, college and pro helped me to gain a lot of valuable experience.

After my meeting with Jenni I contacted Dave Gillett who said great, come on over you are welcome to stay with Linda and I. I sent him a copy of the commemorative book and said I would like to try to organize a bit of a reunion to celebrate the 40th Anniversary of the 77 Soccer Bowl Final and to tie it into promoting the two books I had done. Although Dave thought it was a nice idea he had some reservations about the timing of the whole thing. He felt that because the current Sounders had just won the MLS Championship and we didn't actually win the Soccer Bowl also it had only been a couple of years since the 40th Sounders Anniversary as well as it being a new generation of Sounders fans. I took on board what Dave said, but because I had missed out on the 40th Anniversary and also thought perhaps the new generation of fans might like to read about how it was in our day, made me even more determined to try to organize something. My initial thinking was to try to get the players from the 77 season together, take in a game, visit the new facilities and to do a book signing. I started by taking a look at what the squad was for that wonderful day in Portland and was sadly reminded that Micky Cave, Paul Crossley and Steve Buttle were no longer with us. I made a mental note of the players that were still in the Seattle area and then went about contacting Mike England, Jocky Scott, Tommy Ord and Dave Butler who were now living back in the UK. Mike, Jocky and Tommy came back to me to let me know that they were unable to make it and Dave wanted a bit more detail.

In the meantime Dave Gillett had contacted Frank MacDonald who had organized other functions to try to get his support, he also put me in touch with him and we were able to go back and forth on what he was able to do and how the Sounders might get involved. I went back to Dave Butler and told him there was nothing concrete but said there were one or two things in the works. A couple of days later Dave called me back to say he was up for it.

When I looked at time frames I saw the Sounders had a home game August 20 against the Minnesota Kicks who were one of the team's we beat to reach the final, which was August 28.1977. Another consideration was August 26 when the Sounders were at home to the Portland Timbers but it was also when the they had planned the Alumni game so I decided to go with the August 20 game. I made plans to go out August 15-25 and Dave made arrangements for August 17-23.

When Dave G. started to contact the local guys we found that August 20 coincided with Tony Chursky's son's wedding, so he, Jimmy Mac and Tommy Jenkins would not be available for any of the Match Day activities. Also a big blow for me was that Jimmy Gabriel was now living in Arizona and I had so wanted to sit down and have a beer and a chat with him.

As we got closer to going over both Jenni and Frank contacted me to say that things were starting to fall into place and that they felt it would be a good trip. I was starting to get really excited, I think more about catching up with old teammates, friends and fans from my six seasons playing for the Sounders.

I flew out from London Gatwick Airport and arrived in Seattle on August 15 exactly 42 years to the day that my daughter Michele was born in the Seattle hospital. I was met by Dave and on the drive from the airport to Bothell where Dave now lived I was amazed at how many more high rises there were downtown and how busy the traffic was on Highway 5 and that where the Kingdome once stood there were now two stadiums.

As I got into bed that night I had a sense of feeling I had come back home, because Seattle is where I most enjoyed my soccer!

The next morning Dave shared some really exciting news with me, he told me that I was going to be presented with the Golden Scarf at the game. This was fantastic but I sensed a bit of concern on Dave's face as he continued to say that it was just me and not Dave Butler. Although excited I knew where DG was coming from.

The first couple of days was mixed with a bit of relaxation, visiting friends and going to places that we had shared some special times together. As I mention in Eternal Blue Forever Green Dave and I brought a house together with our bonuses from the Soccer Bowl. It was off of Coal Creek Park Way over in Renton which is now named Newcastle. On the drive over there I again saw some of the many changes and I found myself going in of out of not knowing exactly where I was to then recognizing a certain point. As we pulled into the driveway of where 13042 76th St use to stand, there was now a block of buildings that had replaced our house and the nearby neighbors houses. However 1 did recognize the houses on the other side of the street, that were nestled on the lake that we once shared with them. As we walked across to the house that was directly opposite where ours had once stood we were met with a big hug and kiss from Betty who still lived there, unfortunately Frank had passed away a few years earlier but we had a lovely time with her remembering some of the fun we had shared.

Dave has always been an avid golfer so the next stop while we were in the area was to the Golf Club at Newcastle – Coal Creek Course. It is an incredible course and the views from up there are unbelievable as you look out over Seattle and at Mount Rainier. As we were driving I would ask Dave lots of questions, especially about old friends one of which was someone we had met our first season. His name was Ron Boon and we had shared some really good times with him and his mate Tom. While we were at the golf course David said come and look at the view from the balcony, he told me that Huddy had got quite emotional when he was there. It was a beautiful day and the view was amazing, there were a few tables that were occupied and directly in front of us was a table of four. One of the guys had recognized Dave and headed towards us. I recognized him straight away, it was Ron however it took him a couple of looks up and down for him to figure out it was me and I was greeted with the biggest bear hug. We spent a bit of time catching up before we headed back to Bothell. (You couldn't have written that script)

On the Thursday Dave and I went over to a very different Bellevue where we had breakfast before going over to the Sounders training ground. This was a real treat as I got to catch up with a few people I knew from my Sounders day as well as some of the current staff. We were joined by former Head Coach Alan Hinton who is now a Match Day Host (and over the 10 days I was there I got to know Alan a bit better) We watched part of the training game going on and at the end Brian Schmetzer came over and spent a few minutes with us. Unfortunately we had to decline his offer of lunch as Alan had made other plans. Dave introduced me to a couple of the players and before leaving I did an interview with George Baker a reporter from the Seattle Times.

Dave Butler flew in that day and in the Evening Dave G. Linda and I met up with him and his daughter Jessica who was a stewardess on his flight over and we had a lovely meal at one of the downtown restaurants.

On the Friday the two Dave's joined by two of DG's golfing buddies played 18 holes of golf while I drove a golf cart around with them. Although I didn't play myself it was a really enjoyable 6 hours on the course as Dave Butler slipped back into his other Sounders role the Joker! Before heading back to Dave's we had a nice meal. When we got back we decided we would just chill out and watch a copy of the 77 Soccer Bowl. It was the first time either of us had watched the game in full in many years and certainly the first time together. I think the consensus was that it was a really good game and that we were a bit unlucky not to win it.

Another good piece of news Dave shared was that Jimmy and Pat Gabriel were back from Arizona for the summer as it was to hot for them out there. Obviously I had hoped to get Jimmy involved with some of the functions that had been organized but unfortunately Dave had said that Jimmy was struggling a little bit and was not really comfortable in a crowds. On the Saturday there was a get together organized by Jimmy

Mac and it would be the first time of catching up with the guys, Tony Chursky, Tommy Jenkins, Bobby Howe, Jeff Stock, Alan Hinton, Frank MacDonald and a surprise guest David DErrico (unfortunately Jimmy Gabriel and Pepe called off) It was a really lovely afternoon and it was great listening to some of the old stories and really pleasing to hear that a few of the guys were still involved in soccer in some capacity. It felt like I had never been away!

Another good thing to happen was that Dave Butler was now also going to receive the Golden Scarf so it also made his trip even more special.

Match Day: Both Frank and Jenni had done really well to link in with the Sounders and to get them to recognize both Dave Butler and my contribution to the early Sounders days.

In the morning Linda and Dave made a lovely breakfast and all the talk was about making sure we met all the time frames for the various functions that had been organized prior to the presentation before the game. On the drive into the City I couldn't help but think back to the times I had driven in for the games from Lynnwood and then Bothell and the view as the Space Needle and Downtown came into sight, it still gave me goosebumps!

The first function was at the Fuel Bar at 3pm and as we walked through Pioneer Square people were already starting to gather. The Fuel bar is where the ECS supporters gather before there march to the game and Jenni and Bill were there to greet us. We were introduced to the owner, DG said a few words and we mingled with the old and new Sounders fans.

From the Fuel Bar Frank had set up for us to be at THE NINETY for 4:45pm This was a meeting place where there was lots of Sounders Memorabilia and we were able to display the Commemorative Book. It was really nice as there were a lot of old Sounders fans that stopped by as well as some old friends like Claudia Best, Jan and John Buttle and Pepe Fernandez. It was great seeing Pepe he had been so supportive through those first couple of seasons and he had lost none of his charisma.

At about 5:30 Dave Butler and I did a live interview on a stage setup in Pioneer Square with Wade Weber, who as a young lad I presented him with his trophy at his team's awards presentation (Wade was now the Coach for the Sounders U18 Academy team) There were probably a couple of hundred fans that had gathered and we got a really nice reception. After answering some questions I was asked to introduce the other Sounders players that were there, Dave Gillett, Pepe Fernandez, Bobby Howe, Darrell Oak, Ward Forrest, Paul Mendez, Denny Buck and David DErrico.

At 6pm inside the Stadium the Sounders had set up a table for my book signing and while I signed the books, the guys signed autographs on some flyers Jenni had made up with the mug shots of the guys who were actually involved in the Soccer Bowl Final that day. I think we could have been there a lot longer but we were working to a pretty tight schedule. At about 6:35 two of the Sounders officials Kimberly Aiger and Sarah Tani escorted us out to the sideline of the pitch where Dave and I were greeted by Adrian Hanauer. I had not met Adrian before but had emailed him to congratulate him and the team for winning the MLS Championship. As in his email he told me again that I had been his mother's favourite player.

At 6:50 we walked out onto the pitch where the stage had been erected and Adrian presented us with the Golden Scarf. It was an unbelievable feeling made even more special by the fans chanting ' Sounders Legends '

From there we were escorted up to a suite that had been organized by Frank MacDonald as a fund raiser whereby people paid $150 to watch the game, mingle with us old guys and have a bite to eat. Frank was delighted the 40 seat capacity sold out very quickly. Although it was brilliant catching up with many familiar faces, signing autographs and having our photo's taken with them as well as talking about the books, the downside was we didn't get to watch to much of the game. We were there for a little while after the game when one of the security officers showed us the best way back to the car park. It had been a most memorable day and as the 3 original Sounders left the Stadium I couldn't help but give a thought to Buttle, Cave and Crossley. RIP Guys knowing the Sounders are in good hands!

Back at Dave's we had a bite to eat before going off to bed to get rested up for another busy day ahead.

The next morning I put a call into both Jenni and Frank to thank them for making it such an incredible day, one

I would remember for the rest of my life. It was then off to go and see Jimmy and Pat Gabriel, I think I was just as excited about getting to see them as I was getting the Golden Scarf. They were staying at one of their daughters houses and DG drove Musky and I over there. Jimmy and Pat were at the door to greet us and I felt a lump in the throat and really had to suck it all up as we gave each other a big hug. Unfortunately I was not able to say the things I had rehearsed in my mind so many times as Jimmy had difficulty remembering the past. However it was a really lovely morning and yes it was right up there with getting the Golden Scarf.

From there it was off to have lunch with Ruth Muller and Rojean Siljeg another emotional encounter. Ruth was the wife of Bill Muller another couple I had met my first season and who helped me tremendously when I went through my divorce. Rojean was the wife of Chuck Siljeg another couple from that incredible first season. Unfortunately both Bill and Chuck are no longer with us but if you guys were looking down you both got ' Man of the Match ' awards!

After lunch Rojean went home and the 3 Amigos went back to Ruth's house to catchup with the 3 Muller girls Lori, Lisa and Heather. Pulling into the driveway brought back lots of good memories (especially those 4th July barbecues, with many of my Sounders teammates)

To say the least, it was emotional and there were lots of hugs and kisses! We spent a good couple of hours before we went back to Dave's. It had really been an emotional roller-coaster ride but another fantastic day!

Dave B. flew out on the Tuesday and on the way to the airport we stopped off and had lunch with Jenni and Bill Conner. It was really nice to spend a bit of time with them and to share some memories of our days playing for the Sounders in the NASL. It was quite amazing the number of Scrap Books Bill has that cover all the early days from the games, after parties, picnics and obviously their own personal memories of their Sounders journey which is still on going.

DG and Linda took Dave to the airport while I was able to spend a bit more time with Jenni and Bill and was able to thank them personally for all the help and support they had given me with the books and for making my trip so special. We also agreed not to let it be so long before my next visit.

It was really good to be able to spend time with Dave Butler and I asked him to just share a few of his thoughts.

Dave (Musky) Butler

" Should I go to Seattle? " Ade Webster had contacted me to ask if I would be up to going back for a reunion and to help promote his two books. Family and friends said that they thought I should do it and I am glad I took there advice, because I had a fabulous time catching up with old and close friends, Ade Webster, Dave Gillett, Jimmy Gabriel and several of the then young American guys that were part of the Sounders squad 40 years ago.

The Sounders organization is tremendous, I would even go as far as to say it is on a par with that of the English Premier League! Seattle itself has grown tremendously to the extent that the traffic has become a bit of a problem but it is still a beautiful City. Although I loved my

time in Seattle I had never really thought about it as a place to go to visit but seeing it again I know I will be back in the not so distant future.

Receiving the Golden Scarf from Adrian Hanauer in front of the Sounders fans, who were chanting " Sounders Legends " was a very special moment for me, very humbling, to think people are saying thank you for helping introduce professional soccer to Seattle. Incredible!

I know Dave Gillett will be receiving his Golden Scarf in October and along with Ade Webster it is really great that the only 3 surviving members of the 1974 Sounders that also played in the 77 Soccer Bowl Final have now joined the Golden Scarf elite!

Seattle thanks for the memories past and present!

Thanks Dave and for making my trip special as well! Ade

On the Wednesday DG planned to have lunch with those that could make it. On the way we stopped by to pick Jimmy and Pat up and we were joined by Tony Chursky, Tommy Jenkins, Alan Hinton and Frank MacDonald. I sat between Jimmy and Tony and I sensed in his own way Jimmy was enjoying listening to some of the stories that were being shared. It was also interesting to listen to Alan Hinton who had taken over the reigns in 1980 and had perhaps one of the most successful periods in the NASL with his Sounders team. However like our team of 77 they too came up a little short against the Cosmos.

The weather had been brilliant and Jimmy was doing really well so we asked Pat if they would like to come with us to Memorial Stadium on Thursday. They said they would love to and again it was another thing for me to look forward to before I departed.

When we got up Thursday morning there were a few clouds in the sky but I reminded Dave it never rains on Match Day! And true to form the sun shined on us. During my time in Phoenix I came back to Memorial Stadium twice, the first was for a reunion game against Portland and the second time was when I was Head Coach of the Arizona Condors to play against the Storm and we got our butts kicked but in fairness we had played the night before in Salt Lake and had got a great result winning 3-1. The Stadium hadn't changed and I could almost hear the laughter of Pepe, Big John and Davey Butler at training and the roar from the fans as we won another game. I just thought to myself please

don't ever pull it down like the Kingdome, as for so
many it is still the birthplace of the Sounders and could
probably fill a library with stories. We then went for a
bit of lunch before dropping Jimmy and Pat off but not
before getting a photo with the Sounders Legend Jimmy
Gabriel in the Stadium that had brought us together. I
never was really good at saying goodbye but when I
climbed into bed that night I said a special thank you
for being able to spend a bit more time with a very
special man! That evening Dave, Linda and Heather
there daughter, who was just a little girl the last time I
stayed with them and who was now a beautiful young
business lady and I went out to dinner at a lovely
restaurant near where they lived. (I think I must have
put on 10 lbs this trip)

Time to go home! When I got up on the Friday I felt
just like I did when I go on holiday, I just wanted to
wave a magic wand and be home. I said to Dave and
Linda at breakfast that I think it would be best if they
jut dropped me at the terminal rather than come in. This
they did and with a couple of big hugs and kisses we
said our goodbyes.

There were so many highs on this wonderful visit and
staying with Dave and Linda reinforced that our
friendship was still as solid as our back four had been
that first season!

(I think we only conceded 15 goals in 20 games)

When I arrived home and caught up with my family and
friends there were many questions, especially " How is
it now compared to when you we're there? " My

response was other than what I have said about the traffic and the high rises Seattle is still a beautiful place. As for the Sounders they have taken it to another level, all the infrastructure is in place and they are now the MLS Champions. They are a very good organization and as I saw for myself they have good leadership and good people in the organization. As I am writing this I have just heard the US have not qualified for the World Cup. Obviously this is a big disappointment but what I have seen of the the young American players playing in the MLS is they are now much better going forward but what they have not yet been able to find is that bit of magic of a Messi or Ronaldo.

I would just like to finish by repeating what I have said through out the book it was a privilege and a pleasure to have played in Seattle for the Sounders and coming back has just reinforced the vision that Walt Daggett, Jack Daley and now Adrian Hanauer had for Soccer in Seattle.

Just to say a Big Congratulations to Dave Gillett who received the Golden Scarf at the Sounders Vs FC Dallas game Sunday October 15th 2017. Well-deserved Big Man!

SUMMARY

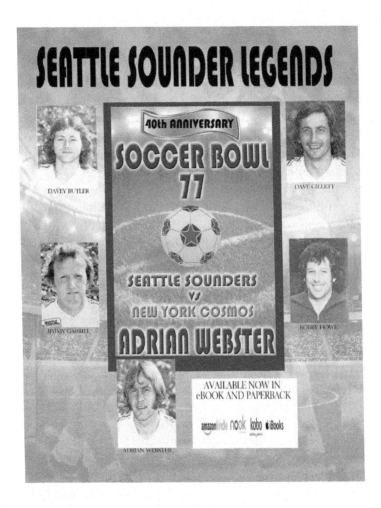

Congratulations Adrian, Brian and of course the players and staff for yet another Fantastic MLS season.

Obviously to lose in the Final was a big disappointment but I am sure that once the dust has settled and Brian reflects on the game and the season he will take the positives and try to build on the areas he feels needs improving.

I do think home advantage is a big plus and would prefer to see the Championship game played at a neutral venue much like in England where Championship games and the National team games are played at Wembley. Unfortunately with the exception of Friel the team did not perform well on the day and consequently ended up second best to Toronto.

I couldn't help but look back to our Championship game against the Cosmos in Portland and yes we were all very disappointed but also felt it could so easily have gone the other way.

I think my biggest disappointment was the day I decided to leave the club which I touch on in the book. I know you can't turn the clock back but I have often wondered what might have been had I been able to get myself back playing to the standard I had reached before my chronic big toe problem and instead of playing six seasons gone onto have played ten!

I was sad when the Sounders and the NASL folded but honestly felt that the MISL was now the way forward for soccer in the US, it was high tempo and high scoring, the fans loved it and I thought it would help improve the young American players.

However with the outdoor game still being the the most popular sport in the world and the US wanting to play on the big stage I was really pleased to see the resurgence of the Sounders in a new professional league the MLS.

Several of my former teammates still live in Seattle and have rode the roller coaster ride of all the ups and downs of soccer in the US so I thought it was great when local boy Brian Schmetzer was given the job of Head Coach. Brian was fortunate to play under Alan Hinton and work alongside Seattle Legend Jimmy Gabriel. What a great soccer education! I'm sure Brian also benefited from working under Sigi Schmid the first few seasons.

40 years on I do think the MLS has established itself as a Major League and the Sounders continue to be a role model franchise.

I think sometimes as a club grows it can spread itself a little thin by wanting to be everything to everybody when at the end of the day how the team which is the heart of the club is judged is by the Win and Loss columns. Seattle is quite unique in that regardless of results and performance it still has an average attendance of 40,000.

In 1977 after we had reached the Soccer Bowl Final I think a couple of things happened that saw the Sounders slide down the ladder and attendances drop below 18,000. I don't think it helped that Jimmy lost Dave Gillett with a broken leg the first game of the 78 season and myself 13 games into the season, also the fact he showed a lot of loyalty to that group of players and in my mind the squad was never really improved upon. The following season the strike was the final nail in the coffin. In reflection what I think Jimmy should have done was to release a couple and bring in a few more new faces. Hindsight is a wonderful thing but I saw this strategy work for Don Popovic during his successful period where he won 4 consecutive titles with the New York Arrows in the MISL. At the end of each season he would let two or three players go and they were not always the so called lesser players but players who had no problems getting another team as they were coming from a Championship team. He some how had the knack of bringing in the right replacements who would then go out and win another Championship. What it did was to keep everyone on there toes!

The current Sounders now have all the infrastructure in place and recruiting is very important too the success of the club. With a Youth Academy up and running it is important that these young players see that there is a pathway for them and I am a firm believer that that the team should be a balance of youth and experience.

I don't think I will be around to see the next 40 years but feel the Sounders are in good hands. Expansion is good, I just think at the National level good leadership is needed and that they need to develop a good working relationship with the clubs in the MLS.

ABOUT THE AUTHOR

Adrian Webster

Adrian Webster played for the Seattle Sounders NASL '74-'79. As a young lad growing up in England, his favourite players were Pele and George Best

In 1977, Head Coach Jimmy Gabriel made him team captain and that season he lead his team to the Soccer Bowl Final in Portland. On the way to the final, he was voted Man of the Match for his man-marking performance on George Best and in the final he came up against his other idol, Pele.

During his six seasons with the Sounders, he played with and against some of the greats of that era

.

Books to Go Now

You can find more stories such as this at www.bookstogonow.com

If you enjoy this Books to Go Now story please leave a review for the author on a review site which you purchased the eBook. Thanks!

We pride ourselves with representing great stories at low prices. We want to take you into the digital age offering a market that will allow you to grow along with us in our journey through the new frontier of digital publishing.
Some of our favorite award-winning authors have now joined us. We welcome readers and writers into our community.

We want to make sure that as a reader you are supplied with never-ending great stories. As a company, Books to Go Now, wants its readers and writers supplied with positive experience and encouragement so they will return again and again.

We want to hear from you. Our readers and writers are the cornerstone of our company. If there is something you would like to say or a genre that you would like to see, please email us at inquiry@bookstogonow.com

Made in the USA
Monee, IL
01 July 2021

72697455R00134